GLADYS AYLWARD

Other titles in *Heroes of the Cross*

Brother Andrew
David Brainerd
William Carey
James Chalmers
Corrie
Dan Crawford
Wilfred Grenfell
David Livingstone
Martin Luther King
Mary Glenor
John Wesley
Richard Wurmbrand

Gladys Aylward

Catherine M Swift

Marshall Pickering

Marshalls
Marshall Morgan & Scott
3 Beggarwood Lane, Basingstoke, Hants., U.K.

First published by Marshall Morgan & Scott 1984
Reissued with a new cover 1988

ISBN 0 551 01100 9

Printed in Great Britain by
Richard Clay Ltd, Bungay, Suffolk

Contents

1. Destiny

In the last century there were many greedy people: mineowners; mill owners; factory owners who exploited the poor till they were little better than slaves. Small children of seven, instead of going to school and playing, worked in the mines or factories from dawn until dusk for a wage of a few coppers.

Today we look on those slave drivers with horror and say, 'Thank goodness those days have passed'. What we often forget is that not all those wealthy people were such monsters. There were many who cared about their employees and built cottages close to where they worked. They donated hospitals and schools to the villages where they lived. They built churches to ensure the people who worked hard for them wouldn't go without the chance to learn of God and all his good works.

In the last century there were more people caring for each other than at any other time in history. They realised, too, that in far off lands there were men, women and children who needed their help. By the end of the century, there was hardly a corner of the earth where we didn't have missionaries – good people who wanted only to feed, clothe and to teach the love of God to those who had never had the chance to learn. Missionary work grew and continued into the new century, the one we now live in.

Gladys May Aylward, the eldest of three children, was born on a cold February day in 1902. She wasn't rich or grand. She lived in an ordinary house with a little garden in an ordinary street in Edmonton, a part of London that was still surrounded by green fields at that time. Her father was a postman and her mother, Rosina, was a housewife. But there the ordinariness stops. Gladys' father, Thomas, was vicar's warden at St Aldhelm's Church and her mother used to go to the local mission hall to speak up against the evils of drink. Mr and Mrs Aylward were different in another way too. They were very modern in their ideas. In an age when parents tried to shield and protect their daughters, they respected Gladys as an individual who had her own life to lead – and Gladys wanted to be a missionary in China.

At Sunday School she had heard so much of the good work done all over the world by missionaries yet it didn't occur to her that she wanted to be a missionary – not then. All Gladys wanted to do was to go on the stage or be a film star in Hollywood. Her mind was changed after she'd been to a religious revival service in a church near her home. It wasn't her own church and she didn't understand what made her go there except that she was attracted by the brightly coloured banner hanging in the street outside. Once inside she heard a young clergyman talking about some missionaries. In the years that followed she often wished that the clergyman could have known how strongly his words had affected just one of the small gathering there that night; it would have made him feel that his work was worthwhile.

Gladys came out of the meeting in a sort of trance. She should have gone to the cinema with some friends after the meeting but she didn't want to go. She could think of nothing but the wonderful stories she'd heard and she decided there and then that she wanted to be a missionary. The strangest thing of all was that God seemed to be telling her that he wanted her to go to be a missionary in China. Gladys didn't know much about the country except that it was very far away, very big and its people looked much different from us. She hadn't had a good education and at school her attention had wandered for most of the time. Her parents had no money. She had no hope of ever going there – and yet, there was no doubt in her mind, China was where God was telling her to go.

Gladys was fourteen when she left school with no qualifications at all for anything. Work was hard to find but she was lucky to get a job in Marks and Spencers. This was not the right job for Gladys. It had no future in it. Most girls were happy to work in a shop until the time when they would marry but this was no use to someone with her ideas.

After a while an employment agency found her a job in a wealthy household as children's nanny. Soon after she got another job as a parlour-maid in a big house in the West End of London. She began to meet guests who came to the house. She noted how they spoke and what they spoke about. She was beginning to get a better education simply from being a parlour-maid. But it wasn't getting her to China.

Then she heard about the China Inland Mission, an organisation to teach people who had little money or education how to become missionaries. Immediately Gladys applied for a place in the China Inland Mission training school. She was thrilled to be giving up her job in service to become a novice in the service of her friend, the Lord Jesus. The studies were hard but Gladys did the best she could and at the end of three months she took her exams.

A few days later she sat facing the sombre faced Principal in his office. She knew she hadn't done well with her work and shivers ran through her bones on that bleak winter's day as she waited for the results of her probationary period.

The Principal looked at the tiny woman sitting in front of him. He knew he was about to break her heart – and Gladys sensed it too. She couldn't look into his eyes so she bent her head, bracing herself for what he was about to say.

He saw the knuckles of her tightly clenched hands turn white. He noted the tenseness in her shoulders and yet there was a strength in the way her head was held. She didn't look submissive at all. After taking a deep breath, he began to tell her how she had failed in first one subject and then another. Her meagre education had let her down.

The worst thing of all was that she was not getting any younger. No matter how long she stayed on at the mission, it wouldn't do her any good. Even if her work improved, she was too old, at twenty-six, to learn the Chinese language. It was a language so difficult to absorb that she should really have started to learn it years before. The Principal was a kind man and he tried to explain that staying on at the mission was a waste of *her* time and a waste of *their* time and money which could be better spent on someone with more promise.

Gladys understood what he was trying to say. She got up and walked towards the door. She looked so forlorn and frail that the Principal felt he had to do something to ease her disappointment. He asked what her future plans were. Gladys turned and fixed her large brown eyes on him. She didn't know what she was going to do.

"I can get you some work," he said "In service."

In service? Gladys couldn't believe her ears. Hadn't she been in service for the last ten years? No. She couldn't possibly go back to being a parlour-maid. Not now. Not after really believing she was at last on her way to China.

The Principal told her that the work wouldn't be as a parlour-maid but housekeeper. Two elderly, retired missionaries had just returned to England from China. They needed someone to care for them in their home in Bristol.

Gladys was shocked. So this was what the Lord had intended her to do, was it? She had been misunderstanding him all the time. He didn't want Gladys to go to China. He wanted her to look after someone else who had been there doing his good work. Now, after all their years of caring for others, they were too old and feeble to care for themselves. She felt stupid at the thought of all the years she had been trying to get to China when it was something entirely different he'd been telling her.

Gladys spoke to Jesus in everyday language, as someone who was always there beside her – a companion. Now she found herself apologising to him for being so silly, with her grand ideas, and she imagined him smiling at her with the understanding of a close friend.

But when she reached Bristol, the retired missionaries were not what she expected. They were still interested in missionary work and when they learned of her ambition, they gave Gladys every encouragement. After all, there was a lot of good work to be done here in Britain. She didn't need to go to China to teach the word of God.

First they got her some work in the slums of Bristol, visiting poor families. Then, a few weeks later, they managed to get her a job as Rescue Sister in South Wales.

Every night Gladys patrolled the city and docks of Swansea, seeking out girls who had travelled there to find the fortune and excitement they couldn't find in their small, isolated northern farms and villages. Without money for food or lodgings, and with only the clothes they wore, many of the girls had run away from their homes . They soon regretted it and longed to go back but they were afraid to face their parents and anyway, they had no money for the fare.

Criminals haunted the places where these girls gathered and it was Gladys' job to find the girls before they fell into the clutches of these evil people who would force them into criminal ways to get money for food and clothes. Gladys got very little money for doing this job and she gave most of that away to the weeping grateful girls to buy little extras on top of the train fare home that the charity gave them.

She gave away so much of what she earned that she could barely feed and clothe herself. Walking around the docks in all kinds of weather took its toll and before long she became very ill with pneumonia. For a time it looked as though she would die. When she was beginning to get better, she went home to London to convalesce.

The illness left her so miserable and depressed that one day her mother persuaded Gladys to go with her to a meeting at the Wood Green Primitive Methodist Church to pray that she would feel well and strong again. At the meeting she heard someone talking to a friend about a Mrs Jeannie Lawson from China. It was the word China that made Gladys prick up her ears. Mrs Lawson was a widow. She had worked in China as a missionary with her husband for most of her life. When he died, she retired and came to England but she couldn't settle. 'I must go back,' she had told a friend, 'even if it means dying there. I only wish there were some younger person to come and help me.' As Jeannie Lawson couldn't afford to pay the fare for anyone to accompany her, she'd had to go back alone.

Gladys listened to the story. She was that younger person. She knew it. God had kept her from feeling well so that she would go to the meeting that night to pray for her health. God wanted her to hear of Mrs Lawson. She had been right all the time. The Lord did want her to go to China and everything that had happened to her had been leading her to this meeting at the Wood Green Church.

Gladys returned to the employment agency that had found work for her before. She would go back into service and save every penny for the fare to China.

The agency remembered her and soon got her work in a grand house in Belgravia with Sir Francis Younghusband. Gladys didn't mind. Hadn't this man been a soldier, an author and an explorer in and around China? There, in the heart of stylish London, she was surrounded by books, trophies and all sorts of mementoes of the land she so wanted to visit.

When she arrived at the house and was shown to her bedroom in the servants' quarters the depression came over her again. 'Save my fare to *China*?' she said bitterly. All she had in the world were three small, copper coins. She looked at them and on the verge of tears she said aloud in the empty room, 'Oh, God, here's my Bible! Here's my money! Here's me! Use me,

God!'

The other servant who had just walked into the room stared in amazement, then told Gladys the mistress of the house wanted to see her.

Noticing how miserable the new maid looked, the mistress said she hoped Gladys would be happy working for them. Then she asked how much her fare to Belgravia had been.

Gladys told her that it was two and ninepence ($13\frac{1}{2}$p).

Her mistress gave her three shillings (15p) and explained that new maids always had the price of the fare paid for them.

Back in her room, Gladys took out of her pocket the three coins she'd arrived with and added them to the three shillings she'd just been given. Now, she had the beginnings of her fare to China.

As she worked, inspired by all the signs of the Orient around her in the great house, Gladys skimped and saved every halfpenny she earned. She sold everything she didn't need, including her 'bottom drawer'. In those days, girls were encouraged from childhood to make a collection of things they would need for their home when they married. Cushion covers, table linen and all sorts of things were made and carefully embroidered and then put away in a big box until they were needed. Gladys decided her bottom drawer would never be needed and the money from this sale helped to swell her savings so much that she decided more must be done. She asked for extra work – at night, on her day off and at weekends.

After more saving, Gladys took her courage in both hands and approached a travel agent to ask the price of the cheapest boat fare.

The man saw her face turn pale when he said, 'Ninety Pounds.'

Only five feet tall, she looked like a little girl standing at the counter. Her black hair was trim and shiny, but her clothes were not fashionable. He could see from her drab appearance that she wasn't the kind of wealthy customer he usually got and she would certainly not be able to afford the fare to China. Sometimes, children ran in from the street and asked silly questions like that and made such nuisances of themselves that he'd chase them from the premises. But this lady wasn't the type to do that. She looked too respectable and rather solemn.

He guessed she must be in service. Maybe it was her day off and she was having a little game with herself. Maybe she'd known her employer to go into Mullers Travel Agency in the Haymarket, making arrangements for safaris to Africa and the like. Well, for a brief moment, this little woman was pretending she too could go to such exotic places. He wasn't very busy and she was doing no harm. He felt sorry for her. Once a girl got into service, she rarely escaped. It was like a trap. Most employers even forbade the girls having 'callers' – young men who wanted to marry them.

Gladys explained that ninety pounds was too much. Was there a cheaper route? The man said there was. The overland route from Holland, through Germany, Poland and Russia. That was exactly half the price – forty-seven pounds, ten shillings (£47.50).

Gladys said she would like to book a ticket and passage on that route.

The man was astounded and told her that that route was closed. Russia and China were at war and the battles raged all round the railway line because that was what the war was all about. Russia claimed possession of the section of line crossing Manchuria to meet up with the Trans Siberian line, and China objected to this claim. The line was closed and no one could get through.

Gladys smiled. She only had three pounds. By the time the rest had been saved, the war would be over.

She pushed the three precious pounds across the desk and asked the man to go ahead and book her passage. Each Friday she would come in and bring more money until the fare was paid.

Gladys then went to another employment agency and asked for more work. She would work all through the night, serving at big parties and banquets as well as doing her work at Sir Francis Younghusband's.

Everyone worried about her health but she put her faith in God and told her friends not to concern themselves.

At last, the hard-earned ticket was paid for and she held a passport in her hand; a passport to China, to seek out Mrs Lawson. But China was over five thousand miles away and was four million square miles in size. In all that vast area, she would have to find Jeannie Lawson. Yet she couldn't speak the language – and Mrs Lawson didn't even know when Gladys was coming.

By the time Gladys had bought the few essential things she would need for her long, hazardous journey, all she had left was ninepence (4p) in her pocket and, pinned inside her clothes for safety, a £2 traveller's cheque. Of course, in 1930, £2 was a man's weekly wage and would purchase far more than it would today. But Gladys Aylward was relying on it to take her all the way from London, England to goodness knew where in China.

Her mother, father and sister saw her off at Liverpool Street station. There she stood. A little, nondescript woman with her luggage – two suitcases and an old fur coat with the sleeves cut out that someone had given her. This was to be her bed covering during the freezing nights on the latter part of her expedition. Tied to the handle of one case was a pan, a kettle and a little paraffin burner. Inside the case were some tins of sardines, beans and corned-beef. There were some hard boiled eggs; a bottle of coffee essence; packets of tea; Oxo cubes; crispbreads and some plain soda cakes her mother had made for her.

Who would have dreamed that this tiny scrap of humanity and her frugal possessions would one day make a great impact on the world?

It was the 15th October, 1930. Gladys was twenty-seven. At times it had seemed that this day would never arrive; now that it had, there were tears as she said goodbye to her family, wondering if and when they would ever meet again. She longed to do the work God had called her to do, but in that moment, like most travellers, she was sad to leave the people and places she knew and loved.

The first miles were tearful as she looked out of the carriage window at the familiar countryside. What would it be like on the other side of the world?

The second part began to be a pleasant adventure. It was exciting crossing the English Channel, passing through Holland with its flat lands and windmills and Germany with its snow-capped mountains, forests and fairytale castles, and travelling on into Poland. It was only then that she began to feel lost and alone. She kept reminding herself that God was with her. Then she would gain comfort from a homely cup of tea or coffee made on her little primus-stove.

After leaving England and Holland she had little conversation with her travelling companions, who no longer knew English. However, people smiled and nodded at her. They were all in third or second class compartments. None of them had much money or they would have been in the first class but few had as little as Gladys Aylward, if only they'd known it. They may have thought that she was touring the continent on a camping or hostelling holiday, but they may have wondered why she should choose to travel alone in winter. Who could have dreamt what was really in her mind and her heart?

Poland was a very different country from the friendly places she'd passed through. Here people didn't smile so much. The atmosphere was cold and unfriendly.

On the 1st November the train arrived in Russia. It looked a most forbidding country. Here Gladys saw people much worse off than herself. As the train sped through stations or when it stopped to load on fuel and the passengers got out to stretch their legs and take some fresh air, she saw miserable groups, poorly clothed and looking half starved. There was no happiness in their faces. Women and children toiled in the freezing fields and streets; just as they had in the factories and mills of Britain nearly a hundred years before.

2. Lost and Saved

Almost two weeks after leaving London, she arrived in Siberia. Here her troubles began.

The Trans Siberian railway runs from Vladivostok in Russia, right the way across Asia to the Ural Mountains. The journey took so long that all trains had to provide beds for the passengers. These were tiers of long wooden shelves without mattresses or coverings. How thankful Gladys was for the old fur coat. There were no seats and throughout the journey passengers sat or lay on their beds. Even their food had to be prepared there. There was food to be bought at the stations they passed through, but only the first class passengers could afford to buy it. Still, hot water for drinks was provided from a station tap, and it was free.

At the station before Chita, Gladys was delighted when a man got on, looked at the strange foreign woman and said, 'Hello!'

It was the first time she'd heard her mother tongue since leaving Holland. But her pleasure in the conversation was shattered when he told her that because of the war, the train was only going as far as Chita.

Gladys remembered the clerk in Mullers

Travel Agency. Hadn't he warned her long ago that she may not get beyond the Manchurian-Russian border? She couldn't believe the war was still being fought. How would she reach Harbin to get the steamer for Tientsin and on towards her goal?

These thoughts were running through her mind as the train drew into Chita. The ticket collector came along and with the help of the English speaking man, explained that the train was going no further. She must get off.

On that far-off day when Gladys had booked her passage in London, she had realised how shrill and immature her voice was. No wonder Mullers clerk had tried to talk her out of going to China. "I must improve it if I'm going to command authority anywhere," she had thought.

From then on, in any spare time, she had gone along to Speakers' Corner in Hyde Park. There, anyone who felt they had something important to say to the public could stand on a soap-box and make a speech.

Even with the soap-box beneath her feet, Gladys had still been a tiny figure but as loudly as she could she had cried out to passers-by the message of God's love. Except for a few who paused to point and laugh at her, most did pass by. Gladys hadn't minded at all. She had been gaining experience in using her voice and saying what she thought.

In the freezing cold of the Asian station, she put her experience into practice. In slow, authoritative tones, she refused to leave the train and stubbornly sat on her shelf, her cases and rug surrounding her.

She'd noticed, as the passengers got off the train, that a number of soldiers were getting on – huge, rough looking men who filled her with fear. She didn't relish their company but if they were getting on the train it must be going further along the line – and Gladys Aylward was going with it. She had her ticket and her passport. This was not a military train even if it was full of soldiers. She had every right to stay on it.

For a day and a half the train rumbled on its way. The soldiers weren't what she'd expected. They were well behaved and although they couldn't speak English, they smiled at her a lot.

Eventually the train drew into a small, isolated station and the soldiers got off.

Almost immediately a horrible sound invaded her ears. She looked out of the window. Orange flashes lit up the black sky. Gladys had never seen it before but she'd heard all about gunfire from soldiers who had fought in the Great War. The lights on the train went out and she ran along the corridor. There was no one on board but herself. She scurried back to collect her luggage and quickly got off the train.

The platform was deserted but at the far end she saw a small building and ran to it for shelter. Inside she saw the train driver, the station master and the ticket collector sitting round a fire. The ticket collector looked reprovingly at her. He'd tried to tell her what to expect only she wouldn't listen. He was probably thinking that perhaps she believed him at last.

With the little bit of English he knew he managed to make her understand – the train would be there, maybe for weeks, waiting to collect the wounded from the battles. Only then would it return to Chita.

At last Gladys understood. No matter how much she wanted to, she really couldn't get any further. She would have to go back to Chita, and the only way she could do that was – by walking! She recalled the many hours it had taken the train to reach the spot they were in. How long would it take her to walk? There was no road, only the narrow, uneven track lying between two black forests. Beyond these rose high mountains. It was late at night. Everywhere was thick with snow. Icicles hung from towering pine trees and hungry wolves roamed in packs.

She was bitterly cold and tired and she had her fur rug and two cases to carry. In that moment how she must have longed for the warm comfort of her parents' home or the grandeur of Sir Francis Younghusband's Belgrave mansion.

She trudged along. Her legs soon ached from stepping over deep snow where it had drifted between the railway lines. And at each step she had to drag first one case then the other after her. For six hours she walked until her strength had reached its very limit. She cleared some snow from the steel rail at her feet, heaped the old fur coat on it, then sat there with her head buried in her hands wondering whatever would become of her. She thought that a hot drink and something to eat might revive her. But even after the refreshing meal, she knew she couldn't go on.

Wrapping herself in the rug, she lay down with her back against the cases for protection from the biting cold wind. She said her prayers and asked God to keep her safe from the prowling wolves while she had a sleep.

By the laws of nature Gladys Aylward should have died from exposure that night. Strong men, better equipped, better fed and in conditions much less severe than that Siberian night, have perished. God in truth answered her prayer and watched over her.

She slept until dawn and awoke with limbs frozen stiff. With difficulty and determination she managed to make another hot drink. After two weeks she hadn't much food left. The hard boiled eggs had been eaten in the first two days before they went bad. The little soda scones were now hard and stale but on that morning they were like a feast.

She walked again all that day, stopping at intervals for drinks and snacks. At night she saw the lights of Chita twinkling in the distance. By this time she was like a zombie. One foot mechanically followed the other. Her feet had swelled up in her boots but she couldn't feel the pain. She was numb from cold and exhaustion. Even her brain was numbed from her terrible ordeal. On she staggered until she reached the station she had left with such determination days earlier.

Afterwards, she couldn't remember heaving her weary body up on to the platform. The next thing she remembered was wakening to a bright dawn. She blinked and rubbed her eyes, trying hard to think – where was she? What was happening to her? She was lying on top of her cases, away from the icy ground. Instinct had made her pull the rug over her for warmth or she would never have awakened again.

By afternoon, with some of her strength renewed, she was sleeping less. With the rug cocooned tightly around her slim form, she sat up and looked about her. Her hands were too frozen to make a drink. Her mind was still hazy. When a man and two soldiers came towards her, she intended to try to make herself understood.

They came right to her and before she could speak, the man, who spoke a little English, told her she was under arrest.

Gladys didn't care. Prison would be warmer than the station platform. Her 'cell' turned out to be a little side room in the station building. It was so revoltingly dirty that its smell made her sick.

They kept her locked in there until evening when she was taken to her captor for questioning. She tried to make him understand that she was a missionary on her way to China.

'Why go to China? We need machinists here,' he said.

Gladys explained that she wasn't a machinist but a missionary. Only when she showed him her treasured Bible did he understand.

He left the office and Gladys was so tired that she curled up on the floor and slept.

The following day she was given some extra tickets and a stamped visa. Then she was taken to a train which was going to Nikolshissur where she must change for Pogranilchnai.

But once again at Nikolshissur no one understood her and she was ignored. There was nothing to do but settle down to yet another night out in the open on yet another railway platform.

The intense cold was making her ill and Gladys felt she was living on another planet. How could people be so different – so indifferent? In Holland, Germany, even Poland, although people couldn't understand what she was saying, everyone tried to help. In Russia it seemed no one cared, not even for each other. Hadn't they had a revolution only a few years before to change all these conditions?

Her mind was so troubled with these thoughts that after breakfast she went in search of help. At a building that looked like a Town Hall she found some people who, though they didn't understand her, didn't ignore her either.

Trying to explain that she was a missionary, she again showed her Bible. Tucked into a page was a photograph of her brother. He was a drummer in the British army and had posed in his full dress uniform. He looked very grand and this had a remarkable effect on the official she was talking to. He became polite and considerate. Everyone began to fuss around her. She was taken to an hotel for the night and given her first proper meal in weeks.

Next day she was put on a train to Vladivostok with an almost royal send off.

'Now I'm getting somewhere,' she thought, and gave a little chuckle at the difference the photograph of an important looking army uniform had made.

At Vladivostok, Gladys decided to stay at an hotel to get a good night's sleep in readiness for the rest of her journey.

No sooner was she booked in than a narrow-eyed, scowling, shabbily dressed hulk of a man asked to examine her passport. Until then Gladys hadn't noticed how people's faces had changed since leaving home. With the greyish-yellow face of the Mongolian glaring down at her, she knew she was really in an alien land.

For a long time he stared at her, then put her passport in his pocket and walked away. Later she went to have a look round the city. Uninvited, the man went with her.

Vladivostok was a terrible place. There were no roads. Dirty, half-starved people stood in queues for food. Everywhere she saw misery and filth.

A tram came along full of ragged clothed men. A scrawny woman ran to get on it but the men tried to push her away. She managed to hold on as the tram moved off again but the men got hold of her, lifted her in the air and threw her off into the road as the tram sped on its way. Everyone in the street began to laugh as the woman began to cry. With filth and mud flowing from her tattered clothes, she dragged herself to her feet and shuffled off along the street.

Gladys was sick with disgust and ran back to the hotel, determined to get out of Russia as soon as possible.

Next morning she was ready to leave. The

man was waiting in the foyer so she asked him the time of a train to Harbin.

He gave her a strange look 'How can you leave when you have no tickets?' he asked.

Gladys was furious. She reminded him that her passage had been paid all the way from London to Tientsin in China. It wasn't her fault that the stupid war was on and she'd had her route diverted.

'Why do you want to leave?' he asked. 'We need machinists in Russia.'

Gladys gaped at him. This was what she'd been asked in Chita. 'I'm not a *machinist*. I'm a *missionary*,' she said. 'You should know. It says so on my passport and you have it in your pocket.'

The man smiled cruelly and walked away.

Gladys alone and trapped in this hostile land was more afraid than at any time in her life. How could she demand the return of her passport? He was the only one she'd met who could speak English. She stood there feeling utterly lost and dejected.

Suddenly there was a loud whispered, 'Follow me! I must speak to you!'.

Gladys spun round to see a girl walking away from her. She was intrigued and followed obediently.

As she turned the corner in the foyer, an arm came out and pulled her into a dark corner under the stairs. It was the girl. She told Gladys that she was in great danger.

'That man is a member of the secret police,' the girl said. 'He will promise to help you to leave Vladivostok – and he will – but not to go to Harbin. You will be sent to some far off place in Russia and be forced to do factory work. No one will ever know where you are. It has already happened to many people.'

She told Gladys to be ready in her room that night. A man would go for her and she must follow him.

Instinct told Gladys to put her trust in the girl and her faith in God. But first she must get her passport.

As if she'd just had the idea, she marched into the foyer and commanded the Mongol to return her passport. Once more she was thankful for the practice she'd had in Hyde Park. Before that, she would never have dared to give an order.

He told her that the passport was still being investigated and said that he would bring it to her room later.

Gladys kept imagining that he would arrive – if he turned up at all – just as the other man came to help her escape. All day she sat in her room, praying and starting at every sound in the corridor.

Eventually, as the dark day turned into pitch black night, he came with the passport. When he'd gone, Gladys opened it. There she saw that the word '*missionary*' had been changed to '*machinist*'. So the girl was telling the truth.

Minutes later the other man arrived and tapped gently on the door. Gladys was afraid to open it. Suppose they had found out about her escape plan. She could be whisked away before her guardian could save her.

Her jangled nerves were at breaking point and she shivered as much from terror as the cold. "God will protect me," she said, "God will protect me." She opened the door and there stood a stranger. In his long mac, with his trilby hat pulled down over his eyes, he looked like something from a gangster film.

He beckoned Gladys to follow him and put his finger to his lips signalling her to be quiet. Her edgy nerves made her want to giggle as he crept along the landing and she struggled behind with her cumbersome luggage.

At every few steps, he stopped to make sure the way ahead was safe. Stealthily, they went down the stairs, through the foyer, past the reception desk where the clerk sat dozing. The revolving door leading to the street squeaked. Horrified, Gladys held her breath until they were out in the freezing night air. At last she let out a sigh of relief but the man a few steps ahead of her was still cautious.

Soon he walked more briskly and Gladys could barely keep up with him as they made their way over rough ground. Eventually, picked out against the night sky, she saw the silhouettes of cranes and jibs and heard the eerie splashing of water against dockside quays. They were met by the girl Gladys had spoken to earlier. She told Gladys she was to travel on a Japanese ship to Tsurugaoka in Japan. Everything had been arranged. There she would be able to get a boat to China.

Gladys almost wept with relief. With renewed

hope she went aboard after saying farewell to her new found friends.

The friendly captain had obviously done this many times for people in the same situation. Six hours later the ship moved out to sea and Gladys stood on deck watching the Siberian coastline disappear into the distance.

She said a prayer of thanks to God. He had spurred her on to her goal. Maybe all the fears and delays were his way of testing her to see if she really was suitable for the work she felt destined for. She prayed, too, for the poor people in that strange land. Years before the peasants had revolted against the Czar because of the very conditions in which they were still living. Some day they would escape from the horrible ways of their new leaders – from people they'd trusted and believed would change Russia into a better place to live.

In the three leisurely days it took to sail to Japan, Gladys relaxed and benefitted from the rest. But she was still very far from her goal.

When Gladys had first written to ask if she could join her, Mrs Lawson had written back telling her to make her way to Tsientsin. That was long ago and she could have moved away. Jeannie Lawson had lived in China for fifty years and, wishing to spread the word of God to as many people as possible, she didn't stay long in any place.

Japan was exactly like the scenes of Japanese fans and lanterns. Clean, brightly-hued kimono clad people smiled constantly. Brilliant banners hung over all the streets where black haired, almond-eyed children laughed and played.

Some rickshaws came by taking people around the town. Everyone looked so happy; the passengers *and* the boys who pulled the rickshaws. Gladys remembered the woman trying to get on the tram in Vladivostok. How different one country can be from another, she thought.

The ship's captain sent for someone from the British Consulate. This was her first link with her homeland and thoughts of her family and England filled her mind. But then the Englishman gave her her travelling instructions – a train to Kobe where she would get a boat to Tsietstin – and her attention turned to the future again.

On the train she passed fields with all the many greens she'd known in the English countryside. Japan in November had trees heavy with white, pink and red blossom. 'Will China be so beautiful?' she asked herself.

She stayed in Kobe for three days at the English Mission. Then at last the time came for her to board the ship for Tsietstin.

3. Inn of Eight Happinesses

There was an Anglo-Chinese college at Tsietstin and to Gladys' relief, the Principal knew precisely where she would find Mrs Lawson. She was in the Shansi region, right up in the north east of China, across the Yellow River, in Tsechow City. Over the weeks there had been so many doubts and worries but at the end of the journey Gladys knew that God had been with her all the way, guiding her through those awful days and nights when she'd felt so desolate.

When she learned it would take several weeks to reach Jeannie, Gladys was eager to start at once. She had a train journey for a hundred miles to Pekin – then another train to Yutsu. After that, old buses that shook and rattled until she feared her teeth would come loose.

When they arrived at the inns for overnight stops Gladys was surprised to discover that there were no bedrooms or beds. All travellers slept together on a k'ang – a raised brick stage. Everyone slept in their clothes into which crawled fleas which bit and itched through the night.

It took four weeks to reach Tsehchow but as every day took Gladys closer to Mrs Lawson, she was able to put up with the discomforts of the journey. She noticed how the Chinese hardly noticed these discomforts. They were a warm natured, happy people; always smiling and friendly to each other and to her.

When Gladys got to Tsehchow Mrs Lawson wasn't there. She had left months before to go up into the mountains. This was a wild, mostly unpopulated, region where small villages clung to the precarious mountain sides – and where no Christian had ever set foot.

Gladys wept with disappointment. She had been sure that her dreadful journey was finally at an end.

The old missionary, Mrs Smith, told her it was a two day journey to Yangcheng, the city where she thought Jeannie might be.

Gladys asked where she could get the train or bus. But there were no trains; no buses. In fact, from there on there were no roads. The way was along rough mountain tracks; so narrow and dangerously close to the edge that only men and mules could walk there. It would take a full day to reach the first village and the old lady wondered if Gladys could face such hardship. Gladys thought about what she had already endured. If Jeannie Lawson, a lady of seventy-four, could travel under such conditions, then so could she.

She was dirty and tired. Her clothes were in an awful state from sleeping on the k'angs and riding on the buses. Mrs Smith suggested it would be unwise to change into more of her own clothes.

"Here everyone wears these," she said, and gave Gladys a pair of blue trousers and matching jacket.

Off the mule train went, a string of eight animals led by their master, the muleteer, and his helpers. These trains were the only form of communication between the villages and towns in the mountains. They took nearly two months to complete the journey from Tsehchow to the far end of the track and back again.

Each night they stayed at inns in the towns and villages on the way. Because of the dangers of narrow, slippery paths and threat of bandits, night travel was impossible.

At the end of the day, it was not the muleteer but the leading mule that chose where they would stay for the night. Once a mule turned into an inn yard, nothing in the world could make him move until morning. There he would have his heavy burden removed from his back, be given food and a soft, well earned bed for the night.

Each town stood within high walls which protected the people from attack by bandits and the ferocious War Lords. The War Lords were high born men with private armies who had constantly made trouble in China from the beginning of time until well into this century.

If a mule train was late arriving for its night's stop, the sturdy gates set in the stone walls would be locked. The gatekeepers were ruthless. Nothing would tempt them to open the gates again before morning. The risk was too high. The most innocent looking mule train could be a well-laid trap.

The first night was spent at Chowstun with Gladys Aylward, the muleteer, his helpers and a dozen other travellers all packed on to a k'ang.

At dawn they were on the way again. The mountain air was clear and sharp as they climbed higher and higher. Down below, Gladys could see the yawning rock-strewn valleys and streams. There was little sound except for the occasional shout from one of her companions or the grating of a mule's hoof as it slipped on the flinty ground.

The day passed, evening came again and Gladys' body ached from the discomfort of her transport. She began to despair of ever finding Mrs Lawson and closed her eyes to say a silent prayer. Just then, the muleteer brought the team to a halt. Gladys opened her eyes and saw that he was pointing ahead. She followed the line of his arm and there, merging into the sky it seemed, were stout grey city walls.

'Yangcheng,' the muleteer called.

Gladys gazed at the scene. In all her wildest dreams she had never imagined anything as beautiful. Peeping over the very tip of the walls, were the picturesque roof tops of the pagodas – sacred towers to China's many gods.

Their layer upon layer of roof, curled up at the eaves, resembled the many tiers of an enormous wedding-cake.

For one awful moment Gladys suspected that she *was* dreaming. Then the mules moved off again and as the tired beasts wended their way along the path to find their night's rest, all the bruises in her body told her it wasn't a dream. She had arrived.

'Please, God, make Mrs Lawson be there,' she prayed. By now she was down to her last six shillings (30p). She couldn't afford to go any further – nor did she have enough money to take her back to Tsehchow.

Safe inside the city gates, Gladys looked about her. Banners with brilliant emblems on them were strung overhead like lines of washing. In the gathering dusk, their vivid hues seemed to light up the streets. Temples of all shapes and sizes lined the streets. Priests in saffron yellow and bright red robes mingled with beautifully dressed, bejewelled people.

Strings of mules were coming in at the east gate from the downward track and passing those coming from the west gate. In the shadows of buildings, Gladys could pick out the huddled figures of toothless beggars with hollow eyes.

It was like a pageant passing before her eyes. Then the muleteer stopped at a courtyard gate and opened it. He wouldn't go inside but he motioned to Gladys that this was her destination.

Jeannie ran out of the house. She was a small, nimble woman dressed in the almost uniform blue jacket and trousers. Only her snow white hair and the deep lines etched around her blue eyes betrayed that she was no longer young.

Gladys was so relieved to see her that she nearly fell from her mule.

The little Scotswoman peered up at her. 'Who are you?' she asked sharply.

Gladys told her who she was

'Well, come in then,' was Mrs Lawson's answer.

It seemed an odd greeting but Gladys was to learn that it was Jeannie's way. She was a hard-working, sincere woman but age and hard living conditions had made her short-tempered and a bit irritable. Sometimes she would fly into a rage and then anyone with sense kept out of her way until it subsided. All the same, everyone who knew her loved her.

Yang, the ageing Chinese cook, soon had Gladys seated in front of a bowl of steaming vegetables while Mrs Lawson continued to bustle about, doing a dozen and one jobs all at the same time.

The house was old and terribly dirty. There were no doors on the rooms, few tiles on the roof and it had a ghost – or so the Chinese believed – so Jeannie had managed to buy it cheaply. It was in the shape of a square with the balconies of its second floor rooms looking down into the courtyard. Courtyards should be beautiful places with trees and fountains. This one had heaps of rubble. There was hardly any furniture but there were a lot of soap-boxes to sit on. It seemed a lifetime since Gladys had stood on her soap-box in Hyde Park making her speeches – and all in preparation for this.

After she'd eaten and washed, partly from curiosity, partly to give her aching limbs some exercise, she went out to take another look at the lovely city now securely locked in for the night against the outside world.

There were a few people lower down the street. They were looking at Gladys so she smiled and waved to them. In the next instant, a clod of earth whizzed past her ear. Children and their mothers pointed and laughed at her as they continued to fling lumps of mud and dirt from the street.

Gladys quickly retreated into the courtyard and ran to tell Mrs Lawson.

'Oh, they do it every time I show my face too,' she said. 'They think we're devils. Everyone here hates us.' She tugged at her white curls. 'Especially me with this.'

'How can you ever hope to convert such barbaric people to Christianity if they *hate* you so much?' Gladys asked.

Jeannie agreed they certainly were the most hostile people she'd met in all her years in China. But she reminded Gladys that these people were born, lived their lives and died without ever leaving the mountain. They never saw people from other lands and the hatred they showed really stemmed from fear. It was a sort of challenge. Wouldn't there be more pleasure in bringing *these* people to know the love of the Lord than people who simply sat and listened to what she had to say?

Gladys doubted they would ever get the opportunity. Although she was much smaller than the Chinese from the Shansi region with her near black hair and deep brown eyes she was more like them than Jeannie was. They were afraid of Jeannie's snow white curls but they shouldn't be afraid of Gladys. Still, Jeannie

Lawson would have one advantage if she ever did get close to them – she could speak Chinese.

Yang, the cook, wasn't like the rest. He was friendly and eager to learn the word of God. He talked to Jeannie a lot and within days Gladys found she was beginning to pick out the odd word. *chan* meant mountain. *fu, foo, kin* or *king* meant court or capital. North, south, east and west were *pe, nan, tong* and *si*. On her way there she had crossed, not the Yellow River, but the *Hwangho* because *hwang* is yellow and *ho* is river. *Nanking* was the new capital city of China. It used to be *Peking* in the north. And Jesus Christ, lived not in heaven but in *chian*.

Many years before, Robert Morrison, another missionary to a different part of China, had translated the Bible into Chinese. The Chinese language was so complicated that the Bible took up six heavy books. Jeannie had a set and from them she was able to teach Yang the word of Christ. He loved the stories and he especially loved Noah. In fact, he loved Noah so much that he insisted it was he who gave out the loaves and fishes. Gladys began to study the translated Bible and she was delighted with her progress. But she complained that she was making no progress at all at being a missionary.

One day she decided to ask Mrs Lawson why she stayed there when the people were so hostile.

Jeannie astounded her by saying that the work hadn't even begun yet, much less failed.

Gladys understood the determination of the old Scotswoman but she didn't understand what she meant. Earlier that day she had been down to the market. The mud didn't fly as much now that Jeannie had advised her to ignore it.

'They're like naughty children,' she'd said. 'Make a fuss and it lends enjoyment to the naughtiness. Ignore them and they'll soon get bored.'

It worked and Gladys was able to walk in some freedom. That particular day in the market she was attracted by a huge excited crowd. Thinking it was some travelling entertainer with a dancing bear, she drew closer to watch and recoiled to see it was a man being publicly executed.

She ran all the way back up the street in tears. 'He just stood there and never flinched while this soldier cut off his head with a sword. There was blood spurting everywhere.'

Jeannie Lawson wasn't at all surprised. 'Well, that's their law. We hang murderers in England. Here, they cut off their heads.'

'But everyone watched and enjoyed it,' Gladys moaned.

'They used to watch and enjoy public executions in England not so very long ago,' Jeannie reminded her. 'And we cut Charles I's head off, didn't we?'.

Gladys was still upset.

'It's their law, Gladys,' Jeannie continued. When you go out again, you'll see his head stuck on top of the wall – as a warning to others. We're not here to change the law. We're here to teach the word of God. When they learn that, then they may change their laws.'

Gladys accepted this but still felt sick. 'They'll never learn the word of God,' she argued.

Jeannie glared at her. 'You didn't think you'd ever learn Chinese, did you?'

At this point she decided to take Gladys into her confidence. She'd put off starting her missionary work while she got the house in order. She had quite a lot of money of her own. Her children were grown up and didn't need it so she was going to put it to good use before she died – and open an inn in Yangcheng.

Gladys gasped.. 'An inn! An inn!' she repeated.

Jeannie laughed. 'We'll attract more people with an inn than we would with a church.'

Gladys was too stunned to say anything.

'If they think we're foreign devils, what chance have we of persuading them to come to our mission? But if we open an inn, we won't need to attract the people to it. They'll have no choice. The mules will drag them in!.'

She waited a while for this to sink into Gladys' mind before she went on: 'With the muleteers under our roof for the night, we can give them good food and clean k'angs, without fleas and lice. But here they'll get something they wouldn't get at any other inn. We can tell them stories. Stories they've never heard the like of – Noah and the ark; Moses and the children of Israel. Stories of the life of Jesus from the stable in Bethlehem to the resurrection and after.

'When the muleteers and their helpers who have heard our stories move to another town and stay at another inn, won't they pass on the wonderful tales they've heard at our 'Inn of Eight Happinesses? You know how the Chinese love to hear and tell stories.'

This was the first time Jeannie had put her ideas into words and she became very excited at the prospect. So did Gladys and Yang.

When the roof tiles were repaired, the doors replaced on their hinges and the house cleaned, they were ready to open. It was a large house that had been an inn many years before, so there were already three k'angs there. Gladys imagined them crowded with sleepers, all dreaming of the bedtime stories Jeannie and she had been telling them.

These men wouldn't only tell other travellers. When they returned home at the end of the trails, they would relate them to their wives and children.

At last the Inn of Eight Happinesses opened and in the evening, as the daylight began to fade, Gladys went to the gate to greet the first guests. Mule trains teemed into the city from both gates, all desperate to be inside before the gates were locked. But no one wanted to stay the night with the foreign devils. Every train stumbled on past the brightly swinging inn sign over the courtyard gate.

Gladys wasn't surprised that none of the mules followed their natural instinct. They wouldn't realise there was an inn there. Suddenly she had a bright idea. It was her last chance. Already the gates were being closed and she saw the last mule train making its tired way towards her. She grabbed the ear of the leading animal and pulled its head towards her.

Drifting on the air was the delicious smell of

Yang's cooking. The wise beast recognised it. If there was food here for its master, there would be food, shelter and rest for itself.

The muleteers were terrified as the team of mules turned into the courtyard but there was nothing they could do but follow. They couldn't afford to abandon all the goods the animals carried on their backs.

The Chinese don't bother much about lack of comfort and once inside the inn they were astonished to see how clean and bright it was. When Yang appeared with a bowl of piping hot spaghetti like dough and millet they felt it must be all right to stay there. Yang was well known to them and no ill had befallen him under the roof of the foreign devils.

The muleteers' helpers removed the heavy shoulder poles used to carry goods the mules couldn't because of the animals' smell. Then they all sat down to a hearty supper. Soon they relaxed and talked amongst themselves. Then Jeannie walked in.

As a mob they made for the door. But Yang soon put them at their ease when he said she only wanted to tell them a story before they went to bed.

Gradually they crept back to their seats and listened, enthralled.

The following morning they awoke on the k'angs to find breakfast was ready. The mules were ready loaded in the courtyard and nothing dreadful had happened to anyone.

From then on, the Inn of Eight Happinesses became a success. Gladys continued to wait at the gate each evening to entice the mules into the courtyard. But as word passed on the trails from one muleteer to another she was able to relax her nightly vigil. The muleteers began to look for the inn where wonderful tales of one God were told.

China had many gods: people prayed to the sun; the moon; the god of the harvest; the god of the rain. Now they were learning that a single God gave them all of these things and more.

Soon Gladys was so familiar with the language that she could take her turn at telling stories. The Chinese language had many thousands of dialects that varied from area to area, from village to village. At this time Gladys spoke the Yangcheng dialect. Later, she knew many more.

The work was hard, but there were three of them to do it. So at times, Gladys and Jeannie were able to venture out of Yangcheng to visit other smaller towns and villages. The Bible stories hadn't reached everywhere, nor had knowledge of the foreign devils who lived at Yangcheng. In the smaller villages people would live all their lives without straying far from the protective stone walls.

As the two mules carrying Gladys and Jeannie trotted in through the town gates, people would stare in amazement and terror. Gladys' skin was taking on a tanned hue from both the sun and the strong winds that prevailed in that high altitude. With a dark complexion, near black hair and eyes, she didn't look much different from themselves. It was the fair skinned, blue eyed woman with snowy white hair that disturbed them. The inhabitants of these lonely places would point and shout abuse at them to try to drive them away. Jeannie and Gladys would ignore the unfriendly welcome as they had in Yangcheng. They would smile at everyone and when they'd found a convenient place in the town centre they would sit on the ground and begin to tell their stories.

Curiosity was always the victor on these occasions. First one, then another, would creep closer to catch what these strange women were saying. The audience consisted mostly of women and children, and once they decided that the strangers were harmless, they lost no time in asking questions.

To begin with, they showed most interest in the missionaries themselves and Gladys and Jeannie were happy to answer all their questions. That way they could gain the trust of these simple people and that would surely lead to more curiosity about this unknown Christian God.

In China at that time men were the most important of all living creatures. Women counted for little.

The only woman of any importance in a man's life was his mother. His parents ruled the entire family while his wife was treated like a slave. Any daughters he had were an embarrassment. Only sons were accepted and if a man had seven children and four of them were daughters, he would say 'I have three children.'

Girl babies were often sold, given away, abandoned or killed at birth. Even women were ashamed of having daughters. If a woman failed to give her husband a son she would be turned out of his home and he would get another wife and then another until he did get a son.

Rich men would keep their daughters dressed in beautiful clothes so that someone would soon marry them. Once a girl married she was no longer a member of her own family. She became the property of her husband and his parents.

If her husband was rich he would keep her in jewels and fine clothes but not because he was fond of her. It was just to prove to the world how wealthy he was.

Poor and rich alike, all women hobbled around on little cubes that God had intended to be feet. Men liked women to trot about on tiny feet like the hooves of a goat. Many centuries earlier an Emperor's wife had run away from her husband because he treated her badly. When she was captured and brought back to the palace, he ordered her feet to be bound up tightly so that she would never be able to run again.

From that day, as soon as a girl was born, her feet were tightly bound with strips of cloth which were never removed throughout her life. As she grew more and more bindings were added until her feet stopped growing. A full grown woman's feet were less than half the size they should have been. With their toes doubled back under their feet they lived in constant pain but never complained.

Both Jeannie and Gladys took size three in shoes – their feet were small by our standards. The Chinese thought their feet were enormous and couldn't stop looking at them.

Everyone, rich and poor, men and women, young and old, wore cloth shoes which only lasted about two weeks. How Gladys hated to see the women, crippled for life, hobbling about in ragged, worn out shoes. Her pity showed in her eyes and this helped to gain the women's trust in her and her Lord.

4. Missionary Alone

Gladys wept as the lid was closed on the little coffin. She took her seat alongside all the townspeople and the muleteers who had grown to know and love Jeannie Lawson. The Camera clicked, recording the sad faces gathered there. One of the mourners was Hsi-Lien, the first muleteer ever to stay at the inn. How he , Gladys and Jeannie laughed whenever they recalled the night Gladys dragged his mule team into the inn yard and he was terrified at the sight of Jeannie with her white hair.

He had become one of their greatest friends and had come to know and love Jesus. Gladys saw him wipe away a tear as he looked at the coffin.

At this Christian burial all those people who had jeered and thrown mud came to pay their last respects to the lady they once thought a 'foreign devil'.

Jeannie, in a bad mood, had for once gone on her own to spread the gospel in Chin Shui, a town little known to her. When she arrived, the inn keeper was too afraid of the foreign devil to refuse her accommodation in case she cast a spell on him. Unfortunately, his fear led to her death.

Like the Inn of Eight Happinesses the upstairs rooms had balconies. In the dark Jeannie walked out to lean against the balcony rail – but there was no rail there. The old lady tumbled down into the courtyard to land on a heap of coal. Her injuries were so severe that everyone was afraid to touch her.

A traveller passing through Chin Shui knew Gladys and Jeannie. Gladys was sent for but it took days before she received the message and more days for her to reach Jeannie.

She arrived at Chin Shui to find that no one had bothered to dress Jeannie's wounds, nor even clean away the blood and dust. The old lady lay where she had fallen and she was in terrible pain. Gladys was so furious that her rage scared the inn keeper into helping to carry Jeannie indoors.

It seemed she would die at any moment but instead she lay in a delirium for weeks. Gladys decided they must get her to hospital but it was a dreadful journey. Jeannie was carried in a litter slung between two mules. It took a week to reach Luan, the only place where there was a hospital. For a month, doctors battled to save her but they could see it was hopeless.

She begged Gladys to take her back to Yangcheng. Though it meant another painful excursion, Gladys agreed. She knew that to die at the Inn of Eight Happinesses was what Jeannie wanted most of all.

As soon as they arrived home, Yang ordered Jeannie's coffin. It made no difference that she was still alive. Even the young people in China would have their coffins ready for the day they died. Just as we would have a grandfather clock in a corner of a room in our home, they took pride in having a splendid coffin standing there. Jeannie had a very plain little coffin. Within days of reaching the Inn she died and was laid in it with Yang sadly closing the lid on the features he loved.

Now, in less than a year from reaching Yangcheng, Gladys was completely alone there with an inn to run; her missionary work to do outside the city and Yang's wages to pay. On top of this the taxes were due to be paid to the Mandarin.

She had no money. All of Jeannie's money had gone on restoring the inn. Although they had people staying there every night, the small charge paid by the travellers went to replenish food stocks and coal. There was nothing left over. The biggest worry was not being able to pay the taxes.

The Mandarin was the most revered person in a Chinese province. He was treated almost like one of their gods with everyone kowtowing to him and living in fear of his wrath.

The *kowtow* is a great bow of respect but many years before an American of high rank had refused to kneel and touch the ground with his forehead. He had argued that he would not be expected to do that to his own president and not even Jesus would ask it of him. Since then foreigners did not have to kowtow.

How Gladys prayed for guidance to Jesus

now, and he sent it in the least expected way. The Mandarin came to call on her.

When Yang ran to tell her of her visitor Gladys was as nervous as she had been on the night she sat in her hotel room in Vladivostok. Whatever had she done? The Mandarin didn't go visiting. People sought permission to visit him.

She went out to the courtyard and gave a polite little bow.

Mandarins were not always men of high birth. They achieved their high rank by studying hard to become the best educated and wisest man in their district. They lived in the biggest city of their province in a fine house called the *yamen* and ruled the area like a king.

They wore the finest silk gowns of gold, red, green and blue. They always stood erect, with hands folded into the enormously wide sleeves of their gowns. For crowns they had small hats perched on top of the head and as a mark of rank they wore a moustache that grew so long at the corners that it drooped well below the jawbone.

From the beginning of the twentieth century only priests and Mandarins were allowed to wear queues (pigtails) but the Mandarins' were longer. Often the sleek black braided hair would reach to their knees.

Gladys peered up at the dignified figure. He stared down at her feet and she shook in her little cloth shoes.

To her astonishment he was very friendly and smiled warmly at her. He wanted her to work for him.

Gladys almost fell backwards and was

speechless from shock.

A new law had been made by the government in Nanking. From that time onwards, women's feet were not to be bound. As men were not supposed to see women's feet, it would have to be a woman who ensured that the law was carried out. The Mandarin said that since Gladys had such big feet she was the ideal person for the job of 'Foot Inspector of the Mandarin of Yangcheng'.

She was to go from town to town, village to village, making sure that girl babies did not have their feet bound at birth, and that all girls up to the age of nine had their feet released. Only babies and small children could have their feet liberated. Older children were already maimed. With their bindings off they would never be able to walk at all as their feet were permanently doubled in two. Two soldiers would go with her as guards and she would be paid a wage.

God had answered her prayers again, She, who hated the foot bindings so much, was to be the one to see the hateful practice come to an end. She would be able to pay Yang's wages and the taxes. Better still, if she were free to go wherever she wished, with guards to protect her, she could carry the word of God to more places than ever before.

Gladys told the Mandarin that she would preach about Jesus wherever she went. To her surprise he said that although he wasn't interested in the Christian teachings, if anyone else wanted to listen to her and become a Christian, it had nothing to do with him.

Yang was helping all he could at the inn even with the story telling. Sometimes he got confused and Gladys once heard him saying that Jesus sailed the Ark across the sea of Galilee to Bethlehem.

'What *am* I going to do with him?' she asked Jesus.

The answer came from Tsehchow. Mrs Smith had heard of Jeannie's death and knowing that Gladys would have to bear all the problems on her own, she sent a young convert, Lu Yung Cheng, to help out at the inn. Mrs Smith was going to pay his wages – ninepence. It didn't seem much though it was all Gladys had had in her pocket when she left London. How much had happened since then.

She had come to China as a very humble missionary assistant to Mrs Lawson. In less than a year she had become the very important personage of 'Foot Inspector to the Mandarin'.

How Gladys loved her new duties. She loved the silence on the high winding mountain tracks. With her guards she wended her way to the little cave dwellings and villages that clung to the mountain sides as though in danger of falling into the valleys below where apricot and almond trees blossomed.

She met with a lot of opposition at first but took strength from Jeannie's words long ago: 'It's the law.'

In Yangcheng the people knew her. Many were now Christians but as she began her inspection they hesitated. Only when her guards read out the proclamation did they obey her order – 'Unbind that child's feet!'

Once outside the city there were more arguments. Men wouldn't let their wives follow the order. Gladys explained that if they had any argument it was with the Mandarin, not her; she was only his servant. But no one would complain to the Mandarin, they were too afraid of his anger. They could be beheaded for disobeying his command.

Set into the mountain sides were caves where numerous people lived. Gladys would call them to come outside and then she would find a bit of high ground on which to stand. Like a Town Crier she proclaimed her news. Her soap-box speeches in Hyde Park helped her overcome her nervousness before the sea of sullen Chinese faces.

Again, when these cave-dwellers learned that Gladys had been sent by the Mandarin himself, they were afraid and they ordered their wives to unbind their daughters' feet.

Gladys would sit a small child on its mother's lap and carefully remove the bandages, all the time rubbing the little imprisoned feet. It had to be done slowly. Since birth most of the blood had been cut off from the child's feet and, if the feet were freed too quickly it would be painful. At first after being unwrapped the little bared feet would remain deformed and motionless. But after a gentle message they would gradually turn from a deathly grey to a natural Chinese browny yellow. Then Gladys would play 'This Little Piggy Went To Market' and playfully tickle the happy child's feet. Everyone beamed to see children wriggling little toes that they had never seen.

When all the children were attended to, Gladys would tell some stories from the Bible before moving on to another cave village.

Bei Chai Chuang was the most difficult to reach. It was eight day's journey from Yangcheng. The track ran out miles before reaching the village and Gladys had to scramble over rocks and hilltops to reach it. Even when she was there, the village was so well hidden in the many caves that she couldn't see it for a long time. Little did she know that that village would one day be her home – a refuge from the evil that was already gathering in the North.

It took many weeks to complete her first inspection. Then it was time to return to Yangcheng and reinspect the feet there. If a child was found with its feet bound its parents would be sent to prison.

At this time there came to the Inn of Eight Happinesses a young widow, Ru Mai, with three young children. They had no home and Ru Mai said that if she could make her home there she would help Yang and Lu Yang Cheng while Gladys was away. So Gladys could travel far and wide without worrying about the work at the inn.

All over that part of the province the people began to look forward to her visits. There wasn't much foot inspecting to do after the first two visits as everyone agreed it had been a foolish custom. When Gladys visited, although still Foot Inspector to the Mandarin of Yangcheng, she was thought of as a friend and they loved the stories she told. More and more were converted to Christianity. This was when she got her new name – Ai weh-deh, the Small Woman. Others called her Ai weh-te, the virtuous woman. Gladys began to think of herself as Ai weh-deh and at times forgot she was Gladys May Aylward from London.

The Mandarin became one of her closest friends. His faith in her ability was so great that one day he asked her to go and stop a riot in the prison. Ai weh-deh reminded him that her name meant 'the small woman'. How could a small woman like her stop a bunch of criminals from murdering each other?

Everyone in the city could hear the horrible sounds coming over the prison walls. As the prisoners were killing their guards and each other the screams of the injured and terror-stricken sent chills through the blood.

The Mandarin explained that the prison governor had sent for Ai weh-deh because in all her stories she preached of how good the Christian God was. If her stories were true, her God would keep her from harm.

Gladys couldn't deny this. If she wanted to keep their faith the only way was for her to go amongst the howling mob on the other side of the high prison wall.

The governor opened the gate and pushed her inside. There she stood, feeling smaller than ever. The prison yard was filthy. All around lay bodies with horrific injuries. There was blood all over the ground, up the walls and on the gates.

The prisoners were like vicious animals. Some in wooden cages at the far end of the yard were fighting to get out of the cages. Immediately in front of her was a fighting, snarling group.

A man struggled free and ran, followed by a huge man wielding a hatchet. The terrified man hid behind Ai weh-deh. On his pursuer came. It was the shock of seeing the small woman standing there that stopped him in his tracks.

She called on her dearest friend, Jesus, to tell her what to do while the great brute stared wild-eyed. Gladys swallowed hard, took a deep breath and in her loudest soap-box voice commanded him to put down the hatchet.

Meekly he offered it to her. She took it from him, trying to ignore the blood dripping from the blade.

The other prisoners seemed to freeze at the spectacle of this little woman, standing unshaken, with so much power over the wild man.

Slowly, fearfully, they crept towards her. Some had been in there for years and had only heard of the foreign devils who had come to Yangcheng. They'd heard, too, of the good Lord they spoke about. Now they could see for themselves how strong this Ai weh-deh was under the protection of her strange God.

Gladys eyed them warily. She knew the spell could be broken at any moment and she kept up her fearsome glare. 'Why have you behaved so badly?' she demanded.

They mumbled all sorts of reasons. She asked why they were in prison, and how long they had been there.

Some couldn't remember. They had simply been sent to prison and had stayed there – sometimes for life. There was no work for them and no recreation.

Gladys was appalled and suddenly felt sorry for them. She promised that if they would behave themselves, she would try to get their conditions improved. Then she turned on the governor who had sidled into the yard when it went quiet.

'No wonder fights break out,' she told him. 'The prison is dirty. The prisoners aren't encouraged to take any interest in anything and they are sickeningly dirty, too. They're bored and should be given work.'

The governor had never thought of such a thing – convicts had always been treated as worse than animals. But he had no objection to Gladys' suggestions which were good.

After that incident the Yangcheng citizens became even more interested in Christianity. They had seen for themselves what faith in Jesus had done for Ai weh-deh. They saw what she was doing for the miserable men shut up inside the prison walls.

Rice was the main diet for the lowland Chinese in the south but millet was the main food for the northerners. A mill-wheel was taken into the prison and the prisoners were able to grind their own millet grain.

They began making cloth shoes – and people bought their shoes in dozens. There were many other occupations too. Soon no one had time to be bored and begin fights.

Gladys visited the prison regularly and sometimes, grouped together in chains, the prisoners were allowed to go outside to attend prayers at the inn.

Love for Gladys increased daily. People began to take their problems to her and she encouraged them to pray to the Saviour for guidance as she always did.

5. A Changing World

The years flew by without Gladys noticing. The world outside hardly existed except for letters from her family, 5,000 miles away, to 'Our Glad' as they called her. She was so happy in her mountain top home that she was content to remain there for the rest of her life. In 1936 she became a Chinese citizen, the first foreign missionary ever to do so.

Ai weh-deh was gradually collecting another family. First it was a small girl whom she bought from a wicked old 'child-seller' passing through Yangcheng.

The little girl's plight made Ai Weh-deh so angry that she put aside her horror of buying human beings and paid the woman all she had in her pocket. Once more it was the grand sum of ninepence (4p).

The child was near death; dirty; clad in filthy rags; half starved and covered in open sores from head to foot.

Within weeks Ai weh-deh had nursed her back to a strong, happy child and adopted her as her daughter. As no one knew the girl's name, she was called Ninepence.

Next came a boy, Less, so called because

when he came begging at the inn, Ninepence said he had less than they had.

After Less came Bao-Bao, an abandoned baby of two, unwanted and left to wander because she was a girl.

When another two were adopted – a boy, Francis, and a girl, Lan-Hsiang – it was decided that a school should be opened. The prison governer said he was going to send his three children to the school so other parents in the city wanted their children to go, too.

When Gladys made her visits to other towns she often took one or two of her adopted children with her. But if there was going to be a school, they would have to stay behind in Yangcheng. And with Gladys away so much, who would be their teacher?

The Mandarin suggested that all the parents should pay towards their children's education and that would provide wages for a teacher.

How the people of Yangcheng had changed. Even those not converted to Christianity, who still clung to their beliefs in their dog and cat gods, were willing to pay.

Ru Mai was beginning to help out with the foot inspections now that her children were at school. This gave Ai weh-deh more time to herself. In these quiet times she would sometimes make the two day journey to Tsehchow to see her old missionary friend, Mrs Smith.

Mrs Smith occasionally returned the visits and it was on one of these holidays at the Inn of Eight Happinesses that the old lady suddenly took ill and died.

Now both of the people she knew from her homeland were gone and sadness weighed heavily on Gladys.

Her sorrow was eased when the Lord sent David and Jean Davies with their little son, Murray, to become the new missionaries at Tsehchow. They were quite young, close to Gladys' own age, and they all liked each other from the first meeting. The Davies's were a bit surprised, though, when, forgetting they were all from Britain (the new missionaries were Welsh), Gladys began to chatter away to them in Shansi Chinese.

How happy her life became again in those next busy years. She had the joy of hearing the beautiful hymns she'd taught being sung everywhere she went – even by the non-Christians. Women were treated better, too. They were respected in their own homes and men took notice of what they thought and said. Everyone agreed the foot binding had been a foolish practice. Gladys felt sympathy for older girls when they had to sit and watch younger sisters running about on normal feet – something they would never be able to do.

Wives were no longer rejected if they didn't bear sons, and daughters were loved just as much as their brothers.

Instead of mud throwing and jeering, Ai weh-deh was greeted with cheerful waves and friendly smiles.

One day – when there was time – Gladys intended to return to England to visit her family and have a holiday. But there was never time. It seemed her way of life would stretch on and on for all of her life.

It was a good thing she didn't know what was about to happen in that far off European world – or even in the little world of Yangcheng she called home.

There was fighting going on in other parts of China. News of this came to them from travellers passing through Yangcheng. But the battles were too far away to effect the South Shansi area.

There had always been wars between one War Lord or another. However, this time it was different. It was of the worst kind – civil war.

On one side were the Nationalists. They believed everyone should be their own master and be free to live as they wished rather than be slaves to the Emperor. The Emperor had already been overthrown. A new government was formed and better laws made. The ending of foot binding was one of them.

On the other side were the Communists. They believed everyone and everything should belong to the nation.

Both sides thought they were right and even people in the same family took different sides. Brother against brother. Father against son. This Civil War had been going on for years in China.

A troop of Nationalist soldiers were stationed in Yangcheng. The Mandarin was in charge of them. On one occasion, some Communist soldiers came to the city when the Nationalist troops were away on patrol. The Communists stayed for a few days and then left without making any trouble.

Now there was a third group thirsting for power – the Japanese. They wanted to rule the entire world and as China was their neighbour, she was the first country to be invaded and conquered.

In the evenings, when they gathered together in the inns of Yangcheng, the muleteers passed on horrific tales of Japanese brutality. Everyone innocently believed they would never experience any of these horrors. What interest could Japan have in them?

6. Evil Rain

Gladys couldn't move. She couldn't breathe. There was darkness all around her. There were panic stricken voices close by; one of them was Yang's. She tried to call out but she was lying on her stomach with her face pressed into the ground.

'Praise the Lord,' Yang was saying; repeating the words over and over again. Others joined in.

Gladys was angry. Why couldn't they be *doing* something while they were praying?

She didn't think of her dear Jesus as someone remote. Sometimes she would kneel in quiet prayer, but that didn't mean she couldn't pray and talk to him the rest of the time. He was always there beside her for her to talk to as she went about her daily tasks. Jesus didn't just listen to you when you were on your knees with your eyes closed. That would make praying into some kind of telephone call.

Didn't the people whose voices she could hear understand this? The Lord wouldn't want them to praise him if it meant standing about letting someone die while they prayed. And she would soon die if she wasn't rescued from under the weight that was crushing the life from her.

If Gladys was unable to say these things, the Lord wasn't. He put her thoughts into the minds of the people she could hear. Soon desperate hands were clawing away at the weight – fallen stonework from a wall of the inn. In minutes she was released.

When the evil rain had fallen from the skies, Ai weh-deh had been in an upstairs room with Yang, Ru Mai and the children. Suddenly, the floor had disappeared from under their feet and in a cloud of choking dust they all went hurtling down into inky blackness.

Today air travel is well know all over the world. Few of us bother to look up when a plane passes overhead.

In 1938 aircraft were so rare – much as spaceships are today – that even in Britain, people ran from their homes to peer up excitedly whenever they heard one approaching.

On the mountain-top eyrie where the houses of Yangcheng clung to the rocks, aircraft were strange indeed.

The innocent, simple-living people had run into the streets, shielded their eyes against the brilliant morning sun and gazed up at the birdlike formation of silver shapes. Some were a little afraid, especially the old and very young, but most pointed towards them and laughed with delight.

It was spring. The cold snows were gone and everyone was happy on that sunny warm morning with its promise of a fine summer ahead. The aircraft seemed to carry the same hopeful message for there, on the side of each low swooping plane was a picture of the rising sun.

But it was the emblem of Japan.

As the people shouted and cheered, the planes came lower still and released their cargo of bombs on the town. In seconds, most of Yangcheng was in ruins.

Men, women and children lay dead or dying. The injured screamed and moaned in their agony. Those who had stayed inside were lying under tumbled buildings.

In the 4th century BC, China had begun to build her Great Wall to keep out invaders. It stretches for 1,684 miles across the land. It is twenty-five feet thick and thirty feet high. Every forty feet along there are massive towers, more like forts, to keep watch for China's foes. It took 300,000 men twenty years to build. They only had hammers and shovels to dig out the earth and build the wall. In places where any invader could easily get over the wall, there were other walls on the inside. If the enemy climbed over the first, there was another and another until he was finally defeated.

But in the 20th century, China's enemy attacked from the sky. The Great Wall no longer protected the people.

Gladys and her family were amongst the lucky ones. They were all unhurt. When the rescuers released her it took a while for Gladys to understand what had happened. Then, in the street beside the remaining walls of the Inn of the Eight Happinesses, she saw the bodies of nine people.

This quickly brought her to her senses. All about her she saw terror stricken faces. Dazed people wandered around. Hysterical children raced through the streets. Others sat in the road, wild-eyed and speechless from shock.

Gladys ran into the inn for the first aid equipment. Then she organised rescue parties to unearth all those buried under the rubble.

The governor opened the prison gates and the convicts were let out to help.

The Mandarin opened the yamen and it was turned into a hospital. Gladys went to the city gates to meet the mule trains and ask the muleteers and their men if they would help to dig graves for the dead.

All day the work went on and right through the night.

The following morning saw the first streams of homeless refugees leaving their city to seek haven in the caves and outlying villages.

All sorts of tales began to spread throughout Yangcheng. Everyone was afraid and suspicious. They couldn't believe that the Japanese would attack for no reason and they decided that there must be a spy amongst them.

With no evidence at all, they picked on one of the converts. Gladys pleaded with them. He was a good Christian man who worked hard for his wife and five small children. He helped out at the inn and worked hard for Gladys, too. Why should *he* be a spy? What was there for him to spy on? Yangcheng was simply a resting place for travellers. It wasn't a great silk trading city like those in the southern lowlands. It wasn't a valuable oil yielding area as the shale beds were in the north of Shansi.

But the townspeople wouldn't listen to the arguments of Gladys or the other Christian converts. They needed to put the blame on someone. They didn't know the attack on Yangcheng was only one of many on other places and that the Japanese always attacked without warning like this.

The following day Gladys went out in the street to help in any way she could with the injured and the refugees. As she walked along, people turned away and refused to face her. In the market place she found the reason – there lay the headless body of the spy. In her mind she heard Jeannie Lawson saying, 'It's the law!'

By afternoon that day a lot of people were leaving the city. The prison governor was taking his prisoners and his family to a safe village in the north.

The Mandarin took his wives and his court to a hidden cave village to the west of Yangcheng.

Yang, the old cook, said he was going to his own village where his family lived. Gladys never saw him again but she heard later that he had died.

Gladys gathered together her little band of Christian converts, her adopted family and all the children who had been orphaned in the bombing raid. They left the city and wended their way to Peh Chia Chung, a hidden cave village to the south.

Each day she returned to Yangcheng with some of the converts to tend the injured who were too ill to be moved. From a muleteer they heard that the Japanese were already in occupation at Tsehchow and also at Chowtsun, the little half-way village where travellers spent the night on their two day trek between Yangcheng and Tsehchow. It would only be a matter of days before their army came marching up the mule track.

Tales reached them of killings and beatings; it would be unwise to stay in the city when the conquerors arrived. But most of the townspeople whose houses were still standing refused to leave.

A few days after the air-raid her converts told Gladys that they had heard ugly rumours. The refugees were becoming suspicious of the family of the man they had beheaded as a spy.

Gladys tried to make the people change their minds. She asked what evidence they had. How could a woman with five small children find the time to be a spy? How could they believe that her young children could be spies?

She told the people that she knew they had been acting out of fear, but nevertheless the execution of the woman's husband had been wicked.

She was very worried about the fate of the widow and her little children. She couldn't keep them in her sight all the time because she was moving from cave to cave, nursing the wounded and tending to all the children she'd taken into her care. If they were left to the mercy of these simple, terrified people, she dreaded to think what would happen. There could soon be another execution.

There was only one solution. She must get them to the mission at Tsehchow even though the Japanese occupied the city. They would be in no more danger there than they were in amongst their own people in the caves.

That night Gladys set off with the dead 'spy's' family. The little group didn't go into Chowtsun but spent the night in the open amongst the rocks at the side of the track, well hidden from any prowling bandits.

Before daylight the following morning they moved on and reached Tsehchow in the evening. From a distance life seemed to be going on as normal. Travellers were making their way to the city before the gates closed for the night. With her sad companions, Gladys mingled with them. There were a few Japanese soldiers standing around in the streets. But with her black hair and her blue tunic and trousers she blended in with everyone else.

How different, she thought, from that first day when she'd arrived at the mission wearing her best blue coat and favourite orange dress and had been told by Mrs Smith, that such clothes were unsuitable for the life she had chosen.

At the Mission, David and Jean Davies welcomed them. They said the Japanese were treating everyone well and Gladys began to wonder about the dreadful stories she'd heard of how badly they treated their captives.

She remembered her escape from Vladivostok with the kindly captain on the Japanese steamship, her arrival in Kobe and the happiness and friendliness of everyone she'd met. Then she remembered how the Yangcheng people had killed one of their own without a moment's thought. She wasn't going to take any chances with the Japanese, the sworn enemy of China.

Britain and Japan were not at war with each other in 1938. But if Gladys were caught it would be of no help to her that she was English. She was a Chinese citizen and was as much at war with Japan as anyone born in that country.

Early the following day she took her leave of the Mission and once again mixed with the people passing out of the city gates – some going to work in the surrounding fields, others making their way along the plain towards the high mountain tracks.

Gladys spent that night in the open, too. But the warm spring air was so different from the freezing night spent walking back to Chita and the nights on the station platforms of Siberia.

Before reaching Yangcheng she left the track and took a short cut over the rocks in order to reach Peh Chia Chung and safety.

The following morning the Japanese army came up from Tsehchow and marched through Yangcheng.

When a week had gone by the refugees in the caves were getting curious about their homes. Since Gladys also wanted to know what had happened to the inn she persuaded everyone to let her go back alone. Just in case of trouble, it would be easier for one person to creep towards the city over the rocks without being seen.

Looking down from the mountainside at the ruined pagodas and houses she sadly recalled its beautiful fairy-tale appearance that evening, eight years ago, when the muleteer pointed ahead and called 'Yangcheng'.

Now there was an eerie silence. No banners. No lights. Carefully she made her way through the West Gate. There weren't many people about but the few who were were pleased to see her. The Japanese had gone straight through the city without stopping, they told her.

At the Inn of Eight Happinesses she inspected the bomb damage. It could be repaired. She loved the inn. It was as much her home now as the house in which she'd lived in London. She looked about her, wondering how soon the repairs could be done and thinking about all the homeless people she'd left behind her in the caves. She felt so responsible for them – even for the non-Christians.

'Oh, Jesus, whatever will become of them?' she said aloud.

A movement in the corner caught her eye. Fearfully she turned her head to look – and smiled. Fluttering on a remaining piece of the damaged wall was a card she'd hung there years earlier. On it was printed, 'God hath chosen the weak.' Gladys had added in pencil, 'I can do all things through Christ who strengtheneth me.'

She had just taken it down and put it in her tunic pocket when, from the direction of the West Gate, came a sound that turned her blood to ice – gunshots.

She ran towards the East Gate. It was her only

escape. It would mean going all round the outside of the city walls to get back in the direction of Peh Chia Chung but she had no choice. Before she'd even reached it she could see that the East Gate was already closed and barred for the night.

She turned on her heels and ran back across the city to the West Gate. By that time the daylight had almost gone but she could see that the gate was still open. Keeping close to the heavy wooden structure she edged her way round until she was in the open gateway. Peering out in the fading light she could just see the uniforms of Japanese soldiers. They were intent on firing at some Nationalist soldiers on top of the wall and didn't see the tiny figure of Ai weh-deh as she made a sudden dash through the opening and flung herself face down in the field alongside the wall.

For a short way she crawled, then, when she was sure they hadn't seen her, she got to her feet and ran and ran until she reached the mule track.

Part way along was another narrower track leading off southwards to Pen Chia Chung. It lay between two high mountains that rose steeply from each side of the path. It was really a river bed that could only be used in very dry weather when the river wasn't running.

Gladys had gone a short distance along this path when a little voice inside herself made her stop. If there were more Japanese troops coming to join the others, they could be coming along this track rather than the main one in order not to be seen. Or they could even come over the side of the mountain where there was no track. They would want to make a surprise attack and would surely choose one of these two ways. Either could be a trap for anyone caught there. Gladys sensed danger and she didn't know what to do.

'Oh, Lord, you'll have to decide for me,' she said. 'I'm going to close my eyes and spin round. When I stop, I'll go in the direction I'm facing. Please make me choose the right one, Lord,' she begged.

With her eyes tightly shut she began to spin until she felt quite dizzy. She was afraid to stop in case she faced the wrong direction. At last she came to a standstill. Even then she kept swaying from side to side. Slowly she opened her eyes. She was facing the steep mountainside. Without any hesitation she quickly scrambled up. She tore her hands on jagged stones and clasped tufts of greenery to prevent herself slipping down again.

At last she reached one of the pathways made in the earth by years of trampling sheep and goats. For a minute she rested to get her breath. The rocks were unfamiliar. It was silent and spooky in the dark and she was tempted to climb down again.

Then she heard it. A huge army moving along the track way below. In the glow of the bobbing lights that they carried she could see marching men, soldiers on horseback and mule drawn gun carriages.

'Oh, thank you, dear Jesus,' she whispered.

Safely back at the caves Gladys told of what she had seen.

A lot of the refugees still had relatives in Yangcheng and they were worried. What would happen when the Japanese reached the city if the gates stood closed to them?

A week later everyone was becoming so anxious for news that some of the men went to see for themselves. They raced back to the camp in happy mood.

They had looked down at the city. It was silent and peaceful. There was no sign of the enemy soldiers and the Town Crier was walking up and down outside the walls. He was banging the city gong and calling for everyone to return to their homes.

People began to pack the few possessions they had managed to rescue before their flight to safety.

Gladys and Ru Mai had a strange feeling that something was wrong. There should be some sounds – some signs of life. They decided to leave all the children in the caves under the care of some of the older people. They would go with the first group of people to make absolutely sure it was safe and then come back for the others.

Yangcheng was still and silent. It was too silent.

Gladys had grown used to the smell of smoke and burning after the air-raid. Now there was another smell in the air. A very peculiar smell.

Everyone scrambled down the steep mountainside and ran along the mule track to the city gate. They all sensed it at the same time and stopped. Something was terribly wrong. Where were the town's inhabitants? Had they been taken prisoner and been marched away?

'Clear your courtyards! Clear your courtyards!' the Town Crier called. No one could remember hearing that order before.

The Town Crier kept walking up and down beating the gong. Its sound echoed round the mountains eerily, and it was the only sound.

Gladys and Ru Mai were amongst the first to walk through the open West Gate. For an instant they were tempted to turn and run away.

The strange smell was death.

Everywhere they looked bodies lay in dried up pools of blood. Some had been shot but the majority were bayonetted. Old men and women; priests; children; even women with tiny babies in their arms. The dead littered the streets and the buildings – shops, houses, inns and temples.

The small woman, Ai weh-deh, wandered from street to street numbed with shock and disbelief.

Standing on the steps of the yamen was the Mandarin with some of his court. They too had just arrived back from their hiding place. He was stunned at the fate of his people. His face was a sickly grey and his eyes were vacant and unseeing.

His friend, Ai weh-deh, walked up the steps and took his arm, 'They'll have to be buried,' she said gently.

The Mandarin nodded and signalled for some of his men to come forward and help.

Some of the refugees ran back to the caves for more help and again the day and night were spent digging huge communal graves outside the city walls.

There was none of the usual respect and tenderness at the funerals. Hundreds had been slain and they were simply thrown into vast holes in the ground like discarded rubbish.

There were few tears. The shock and horror numbed all feelings but many were violently sick.

Gladys found herself saying Christian prayers alongside those chanting to their own gods.

With all the men filling in the graves the women were left to clean up the places where the slain had fallen. It was a heartbreaking business.

When there was nothing else she could do to help, Gladys decided she couldn't stay in Yangcheng another minute. There was nothing she could do for the dead but her adopted family and the city's orphans needed her. At dusk she left Yangcheng. High up on the windswept mountain she turned to take a last lingering look at the home she loved so much and wondered whether it would ever be her home again.

7. The Wandering Years

The caves at Peh Chia Chung soon became over crowded. There was another place, much bigger and more secluded. It was Bei Chai Chung, the most isolated village Gladys had ever visited during her Foot Inspections. It lay eight miles from Yangcheng. With no tracks leading to it, it was almost impossible to reach. Because of this, it was the safest place in the whole of South Shansi.

Lying in a circular hollow and ringed by overhanging mountains, even its fields were invisible from the air. There were only eight houses in the village and they nestled close to the mountainside. Bei Chai Chung had so many caves that the people didn't need any more buildings.

The Japanese were afraid to go into mountain territory like this because the villagers were such ferocious guardians of their homes. With no tracks or paths leading to the village the people were familiar with every rock and crag and anyone approaching could be spotted miles away. All through the war not one Japanese soldier ever stumbled on Bei Chai Chung and lived to tell of its whereabouts.

With all her adopted children, the Yangcheng orphans and her Christian converts, Gladys set off for the long journey over rocks and sheep tracks. The injured and sick were helped along or carried on makeshift stretchers.

Many days later they arrived to a great welcome. One big cave that in winter was always used as a stable where sheep and goats would shelter from heavy snow storms was cleaned out and made into a hospital.

Gladys thought the hospital would only be in use until the last of her patients – the ten who were most seriously wounded – had recovered.

No one could foresee how important the hospital in the cave was going to be in the years ahead.

Word of it spread far and wide amongst other villages. People struggled to it with all sorts of dreadful wounds.

The Japanese were shooting at anyone. Planes would swoop down to machine-gun workers in the fields and rarely did the soldiers pass through a town or village without torturing or killing some of the inhabitants – often just for fun.

Even Ai weh-dehs adopted son, Francis was shot at one day when he wandered too far from the village. He struggled home with blood pouring from his hand. When Gladys looked at it she saw that he had lost three fingers.

One morning Hsi-Lien arrived at Bei Chai Chung. How pleased Gladys was to see again the first muleteer to stay at the Inn of Eight Happinesses. She ran forward to greet him, then stopped and stared. He looked so strange and unhappy. His eyes stared wildly and his mouth hung open, but no words came from him.

He was in a state of collapse and it seemed he had lost his mind. With patience Gladys coaxed him to tell her what was troubling him.

The Japanese had passed through his little town, Chowtsun, the night's resting place between Yangcheng and Tsehchow. They singled out Hsi-Lien and ordered him to prepare his mule train. He was to carry guns and ammunition for them for a raid they had planned.

Hsi-Lien refused. 'I am a Christian,' he proudly declared, 'and I shall not carry guns which are to be used against China and my own people.'

The soldiers laughed at him and threatened. Still he refused. They took hold of him and tied him to a wooden stake outside his home. Hsi-Lien was afraid he was going to be tortured but he wouldn't give in.

The soldiers didn't touch him. They did something far worse. They blocked up the doors and windows of his house where his wife and children were, then they set fire to it.

As Hsi-Lien watched helplessly the soldiers laughed at the screams of his trapped family as they were burned to death. When the house was a burnt-out shell the soldiers walked away and left the wretched little muleteer tied to the post.

When they had gone, his neighbours came to cut him free. He was quite deranged and they feared for his safety if the Japanese returned.

Chowtsun wasn't very far from Bei Chai Chung so they took him up the mountain and told him to make his way to Ai weh-deh.

Ai weh-deh got some of her converts and they took Hsi-Lien back to Chowtsun. The men got the bodies from the ruins of his home, then dug a proper grave in the burial ground. Gladys said prayers and they were given a Christian burial. She remembered how Hsi-Lien had secretly wiped away a tear at Jeannie's funeral. This time he stood sobbing with great tears streaming down his face. He went back to Bei Chai Chung with her but his mind never recovered from the horror and he was slightly insane for the rest of his life.

Everywhere there was cruelty and suffering. The Nationalist soldiers and the Communist soldiers were both fighting a common enemy now – the Japanese. But they were fighting each other too. Anyone could be suspected of being a spy for all three armies. And with so many homeless from bombings, burnings and fear of capture, there were more people than ever wandering along the wild lonely mountains with their few precious possessions. This brought more and more bandits into the mountains to rob and murder.

During her Foot Inspections, Ai weh-deh had made many friends in Chin Shui, the little town where Jeannie Lawson had met her death. So many townspeople had wanted to become Christians that Gladys had set up a Mission.

When news came that one of her Chin Shui converts had been attacked by bandits in his house just outside the town, she arranged to visit him immediately. He'd been burned with red hot pokers to make him tell where his gold was hidden. The poor man had no gold but the bandits wouldn't believe him. His burns needed constant attention and Ai weh-deh stayed with him, tending to him and changing the dressings every day. At the end of a week, the man was beginning to get better and it was safe to leave him.

Just as Gladys was leaving, a messenger came to the town. He'd heard that the Japanese were in Yangcheng again and were already on their way to Chin Shui. Could Ai weh-deh help to evacuate the two hundred refugees sheltering in the Mission?

Gladys hadn't reached the edge of the town when she heard that terrible sound she'd heard that morning at the inn.

High in the clear blue sky she saw the silver plane circle twice, then dive like an eagle on its prey. Gladys threw herself to the ground. She'd taken her adopted son Timothy with her to Chin Shui and now she shielded his little body with hers. She could hear the bombs whistling down on the town but she kept her head close to the ground and didn't look.

When the plane had gone she grabbed Timothy's hand and they ran to the town gates. The scene she saw was similar to the one on that other morning at Yangcheng. But at Chin Shui it was mostly buildings not people that were harmed. They'd known how the Japanese attacked and they were prepared. Long before any bombs came they'd made shelters in cellars. Some hid under staircases. Very few were injured. None were killed.

There were more homeless refugees now. Within days the conquering army would invade Chin Shui and Gladys had seen what they did to Yangcheng.

She must get back to Bei Chai Chung quickly with the homeless. Unlike the people of Yangcheng, though, everyone said they wanted to go to the villages high on the mountain just outside the town. Gladys watched them making their way towards the East Gate and prayed they would reach their havens in safety. Her way lay in the opposite direction.

With Timothy she left the town and began to walk across a field to reach the track that would take them into the mountains. They hadn't gone far when Gladys felt the same panic she'd had that night in the narrow dry river gorge. She couldn't hear or see anything but the same voice inside her was saying there was an enemy army on the march and she was walking right into them.

'We must go back,' she told Timothy.

'Go back?' he asked.

'Yes. There's danger. I know it,' his mother said.

She took his hand and raced back to the town to join the throng heading for the East Gate.

They were just passing through the East gateway when they heard screams of terror from the other end of town.

'They're here! They're here!'

Gladys said a silent prayer of thanks to her Lord for saving her again. Another moments hesitation and she would have been too late. No mercy would have been shown to a woman and a little boy alone.

Rifle shots were heard and a stampede of terrified people crushed together as they ran for safety. Outside the city walls ran the dangerous River Chin. People leapt into it to swim to the opposite side where high mountains rose steeply from the river bank.

Gladys held on to Timothy and fought against the fast underwater current. She was so small that she thought they would both drown. But before long, with hundreds of others, they were scrambling ashore at the foot of one of Shansi's highest mountains. Without waiting to get their breath back everyone started to climb up and up. There were terraced villages at every level but Gladys pushed Timothy on until they reached the seventh village.

One of the fugitives, a girl, Wan Yu, belonged there and her mother offered refuge to Ai weh-deh, Timothy, two blind men, six children and some women with tiny babies. Gladys wondered how they'd all managed to get up so far. There were times when she thought she would have to give in. With a cruel foe behind them it was amazing what strength people could find.

Even from that little hideaway news got around to other villages that Ai weh-deh, the little woman with the wonderful God in her soul, was living at Wan Yu's house. Every day people came to see her to ask her to pray for them. The sick made their way to the seventh village and were all given shelter.

For the village's further down the mountain those were fearful times.

The Chinese nation was fighing back with guerilla forces – ordinary men and women who refused to stand by and accept what was happening. They made secret raids on enemy camps with home-made bombs, guns and any other weapon they could find.

Each day the Japanese in Chin Shui sent patrols up the mountain to search the villages where they suspected the guerillas were hiding.

They forced their way into houses to search and ransack them. The inhabitants were dragged out to be beaten and tortured into betraying the guerillas and telling the enemy what they wanted to know. Often the villagers knew nothing but it made no difference and some were killed.

As evening approached the Japanese would retreat to Chin Shui and lock themselves inside the town. Then the injured villagers and refugees would crawl up the mountain and go to Wan Yu's house to be cared for by Ai weh-deh. They were sure her good Christian God would protect them from any further suffering.

Gladys knew that one day it would be the turn of the seventh village to be searched. There were so many sick and wounded in the houses that she wondered what would happen to them. They couldn't climb any higher up the mountain even if they were well. This was the last village and there was nowhere for them to go. There was only the bare mountain from there right to the summit, then a sheer drop falling away on the other side. There was no escape.

Look-outs were posted to keep watch on the track and early one afternoon Wan Yu let out a piercing shriek. 'They're coming up the track! They're here!'

Wan Yu's house was the first the troops would reach and it was the biggest. The situation was hopeless. Ai weh-deh told everyone to hide. Then she ran to lock the door. Her mind was in a panic.

She couldn't think what to do. If the door were locked, the soldiers would suspect guerillas were hiding there and batter it down.

If she opened the door, they would come in, and so many people were in the house that the soldiers would be sure some of them were guerillas. Wan Yu's brother for instance. He was young and healthy. No injury or sickness could protect him. Not that illness nor wounds nor age would make any difference to these cruel men at the door.

They were so close that she could hear them talking. If she went out and talked to them in a friendly manner, would they be more merciful? They were strange people. In Tsehchow they treated everyone well. On the mountain they behaved like monsters. If she went out to them would they suspect her even more and think it was a trick?

For once her courage failed her. Her knees began to tremble until she feared her legs would give way under her.

For one awful moment she lost faith in her dear friend, Jesus.

The Japanese religion was Shintoism and the faith of its adherants was as strong as the faith of any Christian. The Japanese soldiers believed they could do no wrong. All the killing and cruelty was right, they thought, because they were doing it for their Emperor whom they looked on as a God.

'How can the dear kind Lord stand up to the Shinto creed of cruelty?' she thought. 'Not even he can save us now.'

With thumping heart she waited for the loud rapping at the door which she knew would be followed immediately by the crash of rifle butts smashing it open. The voices stopped. What were they waiting for? Her nerves were stretched to breaking point when Wan Yu called out.

'They're going away, Ai weh-deh. They've turned back.'

Ai weh-deh let out a long sigh and sank to the floor trembling. Jesus hadn't let her down. He had proved to be stronger than heathen gods and demons. How was he able to turn them away at the last moment? No one ever knew. Relief brought everyone to tears. Still weeping they knelt and prayed in thankfulness. Gladys prayed for forgiveness for ever doubting such an Almighty God.

There would be another visit for sure but for now, everyone was safe.

There was no second visit. The Japanese

troops suddenly left Chin Shui.

China is such a big country with the biggest population in the world. Japan couldn't keep her soldiers everywhere. They stayed for a few weeks in one place and then had to move on somewhere else. When they left Chin Shui they returned to Yangcheng and then down to Tsehchow because the summer was nearly over. The mountains were no place for an enemy during the winter with all supplies cut off.

Winter was a safe peaceful time for the mountain dwellers. Once the passes were closed with heavy snowfalls, no invader could reach them, not even bandits.

After making sure it was safe to leave, Gladys and Timothy joined everyone else in a leisurely journey back to Chin Shui. This time they followed the steep track. There was no need to swim across the river in fearful haste.

When word came that the Japanese had retreated all the way back to Tsehchow she returned to Yangcheng to see what had happened there in her long absence. With the year drawing to a close it was safe to stay there. Everyone felt the same and came down from the caves to rebuild their homes and settle in for the long, hard winter.

When spring was in the air once more and the snow covered passes were rapidly clearing, Gladys began to wonder about her friends, David and Jean Davies in Tsehchow. She hadn't seen or heard of them for such a long time. She decided it would be safe to visit the Mission again.

They had only had a little boy, Murray, when they first came to Tsehchow. Soon after they had a little girl and since Gladys last saw them another daughter had been born. The friends were so happy to meet again. But when Gladys told them of all her experiences, they could hardly believe it. They said that the Japanese were so friendly and kind. The soldiers loved children and were always giving them sweets. They often came to the Mission and discussed Christianity with the converts and the Davies's. Japan was not at war with Britain nor did they have any quarrel with the Chinese converts.

How strange, thought Gladys, that people could behave so differently from one place to the next.

It was during her stay at the Mission that David and Jean discovered just how the Japanese troops could change.

Tsehchow Mission was very big and there were hundreds of refugees staying there as well as many Christian converts. Because she was a dear friend, Gladys lived in the house with Jean and David. Everyone else lived in two separate buildings across the courtyard. One building was for men, the other for women. It was sad for families to be kept apart like that but with so many there, it was the only solution.

Gladys was first to hear the screams from the women's sleeping quarters and leapt from her bed to race across to their building.

Some drunken Japanese soldiers had broken into the dormitory and were attacking the women. As Gladys ran in, a soldier hit her over the head with his rifle butt and she collapsed unconscious at his feet, blood pouring from an open wound.

David ran across the courtyard behind her and arrived in time to see what happened. There were nearly fifty armed men in the room. He could do nothing and the women were defenceless. One word came to his mind – pray.

He took a deep breath and as loudly as he could, above the terrified screams of the women and the horrible laughter of the drunken troops, he shouted, 'Pray! All of you, pray to the Lord!'

Again a rifle butt was brought into use. He felt the blow across his mouth. His flesh on one side of his face was torn open and he fell to the ground beside Gladys. Lights were flashing before his eyes but he knew he mustn't pass out. Struggling to his knees again he yelled, 'Pray! Pray!'

A soldier pressed a gun to David's head and pulled the trigger. There was a sharp click. He fired again and again. Still the gun refused to go off. The soldier took a step back and gazed in fear at the kneeling man.

Some of the women had heard David the first time and were on their knees. When the others saw them they too sank to their knees. It had a remarkable effect on the soldiers. They looked about them at the women, hands folded in prayer, and paused in their brutal attack. Then, before they could start again, an officer came into the room and ordered his men away.

The injury Gladys received plagued her for the rest of her life.

The Japanese made no further attack on anyone after that and as the springtime blossomed fighting broke out around the city. Within days, Nationalist troops had chased the Japanese away and taken possession of Tseh-chow.

David and Gladys, still recovering from their attack, heard the cheers in the streets as the victorious Chinese soldiers arrived. Everyone in the Mission knelt again and gave thanks to God.

8. Ai weh-deh, Spy

By the end of February, Gladys was well enough to travel again. David suggested that before returning to the inn and her children she should visit Lingchuang. The Christian Mission there was holding a conference and missionaries from all over south Shansi would be attending. It would give Gladys a chance to meet many she'd only heard of and, as Lingchuang was only a few miles across the plain from Tsehchow, it would be a little holiday for her.

She agreed and with some of the Tsehchow converts she got on a mule cart and waved farewell to Jean and David.

It was her first visit to Lingchuang. It was one of the towns she'd only glimpsed from high up on the mountain track as she went about her Foot Inspections. The Mandarin of Tsehchow had his own Foot Inspector to go around the towns and villages on the plains.

They were almost at the town when the easily recognised drone came to their ears and silver streaks appeared in the sky, high over the peaceful valley.

The planes plunged towards earth to let loose their bombs over the town. From a distance

Gladys and her companions watched helplessly, then urged the mules forward. When they got there only a few buildings were damaged. It wasn't the first attack and people had learned how to shelter in an air-raid.

Each day saw more raids in which some people were injured. The missionaries helped all they could but the conference went on as planned. Invasion on land usually followed bomb attacks but on this occasion, with Nationalist troops close at hand in Tsehchow, everyone was sure they were safe.

On the afternoon the conference ended news came of a distant army marching towards Lingchuang. They couldn't be Nationalist troops or they wouldn't need to march secretly. It must be an enemy army – but which?

Were the Japanese attacking from a different direction, planning to take Lingchuang as a base to recapture the important trading city of Tsehchow? Were they Communist soldiers? So far there hadn't been much trouble from them. Bandits then? With so many roaming about that part of China they could have teamed up to make an army of their own.

Panic swept the town with everyone packing to leave at first light the following day.

As she lay down for the night, Gladys heard that familiar little voice inside her. 'Leave now, tonight,' it was saying. 'You must all leave *now*. Don't wait until dawn.'

Still weak and very sleepy, at first she tried to ignore it but the voice grew louder in her mind. She got up and roused everyone in the Mission.

The startled people rubbed their sleepy eyes and mumbled questions.

'I don't know why,' Gladys explained, 'but I sense danger. We must leave at once. Morning will be too late!'

They respected Ai weh-deh's instincts and gathered their belongings to follow her out into the street. It was already too late. The gates were locked for the night. How she wished she hadn't ignored the warning voice. Some were tempted to return to the Mission to finish their sleep but Gladys persuaded them to stay by the gate and sleep on the ground.

'As soon as the gate opens at dawn we must go,' she said.

When the mighty gate swung open, out trudged the poor people with their bundles and laden mule-carts. No one knew where they were going, simply that they must escape.

They had gone a mile when the sounds of galloping horses alarmed them. Everyone scattered to left and right. The enemy was closer than they feared. Then everyone sighed with relief. Children laughed and cheered as, in a cloud of dust kicked up by the horses hooves, they saw a group of Nationalist cavalrymen – the most admired of all China's soldiers. On they rode towards Lingchuang.

Since the town was going to be defended the people thought they would be safe and turned for home along the dusty road. Then they stopped dead and looked to the sky.

'Run!' shouted Gladys. 'Run for your lives! Run into the fields and lie down!'

She had barely time to scramble into the field herself before the first diving plane opened up its machine-guns. More and more planes joined in. They attacked for minutes but it seemed like hours. Then they were gone as suddenly as they had appeared.

The only sounds were screams and groans of agony. Gladys stood up and looked about her at the dead and dying soldiers and horses. Refugees staggered to their feet, some with dead children in their arms. All around, in the fields, on the road, as far as the eye could see was a carpet of bloody bodies.

Terrified horses without riders, their eyes staring vacantly ahead, let out pitiful neighs as they raced up and down over the dead and wounded.

Gladys returned to Lingchuang with the other missionaries to help. An hour later more Nationalist troops arrived and wept openly at the sight. Lingchuang was a town of the dead.

Spring was with them again. The safety of Winter was gone. The enemy would soon be at the gate and it was time to leave for the caves.

Back in Yangcheng she found everyone packing their belongings ready to leave for the hidden villages. The Nationalist Commander ordered the people to burn their millet crops and so deny food to the enemy when he came. They were to take the roofs off their homes and all other buildings, even temples, to deny him shelter.

It was a sad order but it was obeyed. Some day they would return to their city to live in peace but everyone realised that until the terrible war ended there was no other way.

The Mandarin sent for Ai weh-deh. He needed her help again.

Instead of the long, shiny black queue she was used to seeing, his hair had been cut short. He explained that the Japanese were using the queue as a means of torture and many a priest had been hung by his own hair. So the Nationalist Commander had advised them to have the queues cut.

His latest problem was the Temple of the Great Scorpion. The townspeople believed that a giant scorpion lived underneath it. They thought that if the roof were taken off it would escape.

When Ai weh-deh asked if he believed that, the Mandarin laughed and shook his head. 'No. But I alone cannot remove the roof and no one else will help me.' He asked if the Christian converts would do it for him and added, 'It's so old and ugly, I wish the entire building were gone.'

They agreed to knock it down and the people of Yangcheng watched in terror. At the end of the day. when it was completely dismantled, nothing terrible had happened to anyone and no horrible huge scorpion roamed the city streets. To celebrate, the Mandarin gave a feast.

He made a speech saying he hoped they would all soon be together again. Then, to everyone's amazement, he turned to Gladys and said, 'Ai weh-deh, I should like to become a Christian'.

Everyone gasped and Gladys was at a loss for

words but she was delighted. During the days in hiding he intended to study the Bible that Robert Morrison had translated into Chinese. When the war was ended and they all met again in Yangcheng, he would be baptised.

There were many foreign journalists in China reporting on the fighting between the Japanese, Communist and Nationalist armies. One of them, Theodore White, an American, had heard of the small woman missionary living in the mountains of south Shansi. He found his way to Yangcheng just before everyone left and asked Gladys if she would be interviewed. Gladys was so angry at what was happening in China that she felt the rest of the world ought to be told about it.

She told him of all she had heard and all she had seen with her own eyes, of all the brutalities and how the poor peasants were driven from their homes to wander and beg for food and shelter.

When Theodore White returned to America, a big article appeared in *Time Magazine*. Little did they realise what harm that interview would do.

Living once more in the caves, Ai weh-deh moved about from village to village – Bei Chai Chung, Peh Chia Chung and many smaller ones. Christianity was spreading and more and more people were placing their trust in the good Lord who would one day deliver them from the evil surrounding them.

On her lonely treks high on the mountain passes, Gladys often caught glimpses of Japanese soldiers marching along or making camps in the valleys below.

She began to make notes of the direction in which they were heading. She counted their horses, mules, guns and all other items of equipment. This gave her some idea of their strength. When she reached the next village there was always someone able to pass on the information to the Nationalist soldiers in the area.

Sometimes she went through Japanese occupied towns to visit Christian Missions. The Japanese still left these people alone because they were not yet at war with Europe and America. Gladys made careful note of troop movements. Were they preparing to leave the town? In which direction were they going?

Without realising it, Ai weh-deh had become a spy. As a Chinese citizen she considered it her right to do this to protect *her* country from attacks.

Friends worried in case she stumbled on the mountain paths. She could break a leg or do some other terrible injury and no one would know where she was or even be aware that she was missing. She could even be lying dead somewhere while they thought she was on her way from one village to the next.

Gladys argued that it was safer to go alone and on foot. She could crouch behind rocks, lie flat and hide amongst the crags. A mule couldn't be hidden like that.

In the caves little groups of orphans arrived every day from towns, cities and villages. Gladys hadn't even heard of some of the places – but everyone had heard of Ai weh-deh.

The Japanese were making another attempt to recapture Tsehchow. Fighting was so fierce that the Mission was overflowing with refugees and orphans. The Nationalist soldiers who were stationed there were also bringing in their wounded and the entire town was packed with people. Gladys thought she should go to help Jean and David.

When she saw the number of orphans there she sent a letter to the authorities. She said that the Japanese had showed kindness during their first occupation but now that Tsehchow was so fiercely defended, the enemy soldiers wouldn't be very friendly and kind if they succeeded in occupying it again. She asked what could be done to safeguard the children.

A reply told her to send the children to Sian in the far south, across the Yellow River, where Madame Chiang Kai-shek, wife of the Nationalist General, had set up a big orphanage. One of the converts volunteered to take a bei (a hundred) of children. Safe in Sian, he sent word he was coming back for more. Gladys waited and waited but he never returned to Tsehchow. The Japanese had captured and killed him on the way.

One night, after prayers at the Mission, one of the Christian convert soldiers waited to speak to her after the others had left. Thinking he had some personal problem he wanted to discuss, Ai weh-deh smiled, but her smile faded when she read the note he gave her. It was a warning from his commander. Ai weh-deh was in great danger and she must go with the soldier who would lead her to safety.

Gladys couldn't understand why she should be in any more danger than anyone else in the town. She refused to go. She said that she had too much work to do.

Unknown to her, a copy of American *Time Magazine* containing her interview with the journalist had fallen into Japanese hands.

All that night she couldn't sleep. That same little voice was warning her of danger. At Lingchuang she'd ignored it and regretted it later. But what danger? If the enemy captured the city, *everyone* would be in danger.

The following day the battle was getting closer and people were already fleeing from the city – the one place where they'd believed they were safe. The wounded were evacuted first, to the hidden cave village, because the Japanese shot the wounded – even their own.

Exhausted, and still dressed, Ai weh-deh sank on to her bed that night. She badly needed rest after not sleeping the previous night and she faced another hard day.

Suddenly something hit the window and she was wide awake. There it was again. She got up and crept across the room to peep out. It was the soldier again, throwing little pieces of gravel at the glass to attract her attention.

'You must retreat with the soldiers at once,' he said.

'Oh, why me? I'm tired,' Gladys argued irritably.

The soldier handed her another piece of

paper. 'These are being pasted on the walls in all the villages,' he said. 'It's only a matter of time before you are betrayed. There are spies everywhere.'

Gladys sent him away and then unfolded the paper and held it to the lamp to see. It was a list of wanted people and there was a hundred dollars reward for any one of them captured alive.

The first name was the Mandarin of Tsehchow and then some others Gladys didn't know. The last name was – 'The Small Woman known as Ai weh-deh'.

The words danced before her eyes. Had she been exposed as a spy? She was a spy but for her own country and had betrayed no one. Clearly her whereabouts were unknown to the enemy – so far.

She wasn't a coward and had refused to run away and leave all the others to the mercy of the cruel foe who would march through the gates at any time.

Yet, what good would she do anyone to stay in order to be captured and executed? That could prove more dangerous for the Tsehchow people, and especially for those in the Mission who were harbouring her.

'Oh, dear Lord, what would you have me do, run away or stay and be killed?

A Christian missionary spy would be a prize for the Japanese to make an example of. She had seen the results of their horrific tortures. In their hands, death could be a welcome release.

She said a little prayer she'd learned years

earlier: 'If I must die let me be not afraid of death. But, oh, God let there be a reason for my dying.'

She began to collect and burn all her personal papers and letters. If she decided to leave there must be nothing left behind to say she had ever been at the Mission. She picked up her treasured Bible and hesitated for a moment. That must go with her, no matter what. She fingered it lovingly and when it fell open, she read the paragraph where her thumb rested. 'Flee ye! Flee ye into the mountains! Dwell deeply in the hidden places because the King of Babylon has conceived a purpose against you!'

Then she really knew what her Lord wanted for her – life not a fruitless death. There must be work for her somewhere else. She took one more look at the poster the soldier had brought and, clutching only that and her Bible, she left the building. There was no one in the courtyard except an elderly convert. Gladys showed him the poster. 'You understand why I must go, don't you?'

The man sadly shook his head. 'You should have gone before now!'

Without waiting for an explanation she ran across the yard to the Mission Gate where the gateman was just coming on duty and asked him to bring her mule as she was leaving.

He didn't speak but pointed to the little spy-hole in the gate which looked out on the street towards the city gate. It had just swung open for the day and the gateway was filled with enemy soldiers.

Gladys felt her feet were glued to the ground. Mao, the gateman pushed her from the gate and yelled, 'Run! Run!'

She felt as though that word would echo through her head for the rest of her life – if there was to be a rest of her life.

Gladys ran from the courtyard through the back gate into the graveyard, and straight into full view of another group of soldiers coming from another direction. Before she could get out of sight they opened fire. She threw herself flat on the ground. Still the shots rang out. She doubted if they knew they were shooting at The Small Woman known as Ai weh-deh with a price of one hundred dollars on her head. They would fire at anyone.

As these ideas ran through her mind, there was a severe thump between her shoulders, followed by a red-hot burning sensation, and she knew she was shot.

The soldiers rarely checked if their target was alive or dead but this time they continued to fire. There was some long corn close to where she lay and Gladys managed to struggle out of her coat and wriggle into the grain while bullets slammed into the discarded garment.

She lay still, despite the burning pain in her back. Eventually the soldiers got bored and went away. Gladys felt strange. The earth beneath her face seemed to come close and then fade away in a blur. Her eyes refused to focus and her last thoughts were, 'I'm dying! Oh, dear Jesus, I'm dying!'

The sun was warm on her skin and she slowly

opened her eyes. Everywhere was quiet. With the sun high above she knew it was afternoon. She must have been unconscious since dawn. The pain was still there. Carefully she felt the wound. The bullet had only scraped the skin away without penetrating her body and she'd lost no blood.

Come night the enemy would lock themselves in the city and she could make her escape.

While she lay there she made plans. The bei (hundred) of orphans the convert took to Sian were safe now. She worried for those left behind in Tsehchow but she could do nothing to help them. Even if she could steal back into the city it would be unsafe for the children to be found with The Small Woman known as Ai weh-deh.

At night she began to move slowly and painfully through the field towards the plain.

By dawn she had reached the seclusion of the mountains she knew so well. From there she made her way back to her children – Ninepence, Less, Bao-Bao, Lan Hsiang, Timothy and the orphans.

It took three days to get to them. She was weary and in pain when she arrived but there was such a welcome. No one had known if she were dead or alive and they were so relieved to see her. Her wound was dressed and after a meal Gladys slept and slept for a whole day.

9. The Long Walk

In her absence the number of orphans had increased even more.

After her refreshing sleep, Gladys told Ru Mai of the plan she'd made while lying in the field at Tsehchow. The children must go to Sian to Madame Chiang Kai-shek.

That night the very young children were sent to bed early with the promise of being taken for a long walk the next day. The older ones helped Ai weh-deh and Ru Mai to collect what little food could be spared by the refugees. They had no money but hoped to find food in villages along the way.

They gathered all the cloth shoes they could find and tied them into little bundles for each child to carry. They would wear out many pairs in the next weeks.

When all was ready, Gladys and Ru Mai knelt with all the cave dwellers and prayed to the Lord for a safe journey. Then they went to sleep in readiness for the great ordeal facing them. Her back still hurt but Gladys was certain the Lord would provide her with all the strength she would need.

Next day, at first light, everyone was ready.

The youngest thought it was a picnic and were so excited that they raced about and chased each other. Ai weh-deh begged them to stop. They would tire themselves out. But with so many happy laughing voices she couldn't make herself heard.

Eventually she blew a whistle and there was some order while she took a roll-call – something she was to do often in the following weeks. Off they set in the longest crocodile anyone had ever seen. Ai weh-deh went first and Ru Mai brought up the rear with her own three children. Older children were posted at intervals to keep the little ones under control. Everyone who was able carried a tiny child.

On and on they marched. Young ones hopped over rocks and ran up the mountainside, making sweeping arcs back to the path. Every few miles they stopped for a rest and for something to eat. Food was rationed because it was to last until they found more – and no one could be sure when that would be.

By late afternoon the little ones were weary and cried to go home. No one had the heart to tell them they must walk on.

Gladys had one consolation. If Foot Binding were still the law, these children wouldn't have been able to escape.

It was dark when they reached the first village, where they were given food. But the only place for so many to sleep was in an old disused temple. It was filled with rats but everyone was too tired to care.

Next day came and went without sight of a

village or food and they slept out in the open. It rained in the night and everyone awoke cold and soaking wet.

They walked all that day until evening when they met an old man on the path. He led them to his village. There was plenty of food and they were all taken into different houses to sleep on warm k'angs.

After roll-call the following morning they were off again. Shoes were wearing thin and the soles, made of tree bark were becoming dangerously slippy so they were thrown away and new ones taken from the bundles. Some had lost the little bundles they'd been carrying but there were enough new shoes to go round.

From then on every night was spent without shelter but the nights were warm. Day after day they walked on. Hunger and thirst were with them constantly. Children were always wailing in misery and weariness. Feet hurt. Children fell and hurt themselves. They asked questions all the time. Occasionally thirst was satisfied when they found water trickling from rocks and they cupped their hands to catch the drops.

Gladys was beginning to feel ill from the bullet wound and all the worry she had. Once she stopped and turned to look behind her. All along the narrow path, stretching out of sight round the winding mountain pass, she saw children – children – children of all ages and sizes. She sighed and whispered, 'Oh, dear Lord, why did you land me with all these children?'

One of the older ones must have read her thoughts. 'Fear ye not little flock,' he said.

Gladys smiled at him and then turned and continued on her way.

Exactly one week from starting out, she was just looking for somewhere to stop for the night when some children pointed ahead and shouted, 'Soldiers! Soldiers!'

Her heart sank. If she ordered them all to scatter and hide amongst the rocks, she may never collect them all together again. Some were bound to get lost. She shielded her eyes against the evening sun and saw – Nationalist uniforms.

Everyone forgot their sore feet and ran forward . There were fifty soldiers with plenty of food supplies. They camped with the orphans and, with such a guard, everyone felt really safe that night.

More terrible days lay ahead – blistered, swollen feet; sun burnt skin; lips cracked and mouths swollen from thirst. To cheer them up, Gladys encouraged them to sing the hymns she'd taught them. Their small piping voices echoed round the mountains and along the trail. Then she worried in case they were heard by the enemy.

It was twelve days after starting out that Gladys, on rounding a bend on the track, stopped and gazed down into the valley. Immediately below was a village and, way ahead, in the far distance, she saw the setting sun glistening and dancing on water – Hwang Ho, The Yellow River.

Although it would be another day's march to reach it, their hearts lightened. That night they would sleep under a roof and have food from the village.

But the village was deserted except for one old man. He said that the Japanese were coming through the valley and everyone had fled. His family had all been killed by the enemy and he didn't care what happened to him. Anyway, he was too old to run. He told them the last boat had gone from that side of the river. There would be no more.

'Rubbish!' thought Gladys and off the marchers went again. Now the children really felt like singing as the river grew ever closer. Once on the boat, all their troubles would be over.

It was the middle of the night when they reached the river bank but the moonlight was as bright as day. Children ran to the waters edge to splash in the shallows. They moved on to the ferry-stage but there were no boats.

Gladys comforted them saying, 'The last boat has gone for tonight but if we stay here we'll be on the first one tomorrow.'

After prayers they all lay down to sleep. Her back was burning like fire and Gladys could only lie on her side.

Morning came but no boat crossed the river. Gladys felt feverish and she was sick from hunger. She wondered if there was any food in the village they'd passed the night before. Some older boys went to look. They found some stale, mouldy food and there was only enough for the young ones; nothing for themselves, Gladys or Ru Mai.

At night the children were hungry again and

all crying. They were told stories and everyone sang hymns.

Four more days went by without food.

The children had never seen a river before and all they knew of this river was the shallow water at the edge. One child gazed at the mile of water between themselves and the far bank and asked, 'Can't we walk across?'

Ai weh-deh explained how deep it was and thought wryly, 'They have the wrong guide. *I* can't walk on water.'

The Yellow River often flooded in the summertime and at one flooding one million valley people lost their lives. It is 2,600 miles long and over the centuries has changed its course ten times. Because of all this it is known as China's Sorrow. It had become Ai weh-deh's sorrow, too.

Sualan, one of the bigger girls stood beside her and said, 'Do you remember Moses, Ai weh-deh? God opened the Red Sea to let him take the children of Israel across.'

Gladys was feeling irritable and snapped, 'I'm not Moses!'

'But *God* is God. Why doesn't he do it for *us*?'

Ai weh-deh had no answer for her. She turned to the pitiful children and wondered if it had all been a mistake, and she should not have brought them there. Again she gathered them together to sing and keep their minds off food.

There was a humming in the air and the Nationalist officer stopped his patrol. Was it a Japanese plane? The humming came no closer and it seemed to be on the ground a little way ahead. It sounded like singing.

He climbed a bit of a rise and looked through his binoculars to see a mass of children, sitting in a circle – singing. He couldn't believe his eyes. It must be some enemy trick. He crept closer to peer through the riverside reeds.

Some little ones saw him and, shouting excitedly, they ran and surrounded him. He went to ask Gladys what they were doing there. Who were they? How did they get there? Didn't they know the Japanese would be there at any moment?

Gladys struggled to her feet and almost fell over.

'Are you ill?' he asked.

She shook her head and said she was all right. Then she answered all his questions. He promised to get them across the river but it would be dangerous. If an enemy plane came whilst they were in mid river, it would fire on them.

With his fingers in his mouth he whistled across the mile stretch and received an immediate reply. Then a small boat set out from the opposite bank. It wasn't the big ferry and it had to make three trips to get everyone across. Gladys and Sualan went in the third boat load.

Gladys looked down as the little boats prow cut through and parted the waters. She smiled at Sualan but they said nothing.

They ate and slept in a village near the river bank and then the following day they walked on to Mien Chih where a bombed-out temple was being used by a refugee organisation. Gladys took the children to a pond where they washed their clothes for the first time since leaving home.

Next morning they boarded a train that would take them south towards Sian. They had no money for tickets but all trains were free to refugees. The children had never seen a train before. When the great engine steamed into the station they thought it was a dragon and they all screamed and ran.

It took ages to find them but after a roll-call they were all put aboard. When they came to a tunnel everyone screamed in terror again.

They were on that train for four days, getting food from refugee organisations at the stations they stopped at.

It seemed all their problems were behind them – until, at Tiensan, they discovered that a railway bridge had been bombed and there was no line. Gladys remembered what had happened at Chita. At least it was springtime here and there was no snow.

All the passengers, young and old, would have to climb up the steep face of a mountain and down the far side where the line continued. Gladys felt she just couldn't go on and she prayed to Jesus for strength to reach Madame Chiang Kai-shek in Sian.

All the shoes were worn out by this time, but they struggled on, sleeping in sandy caves at night. The tired little ones cried to be carried and Gladys thought they would never survive. She had let them all down. In utter misery she sat on a rock and burst into tears. Everyone else did the same.

When she heard all the sobbing, even from Ru Mai, she looked about her and thought, 'Well, a good cry never harmed anyone!'

Then she got to her feet and marched on, singing a cheery song. They all joined in and as they got to the mountain peak they looked down and saw several villages like those at Chin Shui.

It took five days to cross that mountain, but at last they reached Tung Kwan where there was a big refugee organisation and – a railway line.

But *there were no trains*. The line ran by the Yellow River where the Japanese were stationed, and only coal trains were allowed to go by. They would have to walk all the way to Sian.

After three weeks of sore feet; carrying wailing, complaining children; of pain, hunger, thirst, lack of sleep and worry, Gladys was feeling ill and bad tempered. When two men roused her from her sleep she said, 'Oh, leave me alone! Go away!'

She was ashamed of her outburst when they said they could hide her and all the children on the coal train and get them away.

The organisation people, Gladys, Ru Mai and all the big children made a human chain, right along to the station. Sleeping children were passed from one person to the next and packed in bedding bundles on the trucks amongst the hard black coal.

The Chinese are a hardy race, particularly the mountain dwellers and when the children awoke next morning all aches and pains were forgotten. They couldn't stop laughing when they saw where they were and how everyone had turned black in the night.

Gladys thought of the days it would have taken to walk to Sian and she knew she wouldn't have had the strength. She thanked God for the beautiful, dirty coal.

The lowland city to which the train took them was even more fairy-tale like than Yangcheng had been. Beautiful pagodas were everywhere. Almond, cherry and apricot trees were in full blossom. Delicate little bridges crossed cool, clear streams.

Then there were more trains, for six days and nights, until finally they arrived at the massive city of Sian.

It was midday but the city gate was closed. A man looked down from the stone wall at the bei of children and called, 'The city is closed to all refugees.'

There just wasn't room for any more refugees. They must camp in the street beside the wall.

Gladys was in such despair that she leant her head against the wooden gate and wept.

That night some other refugees told her of a big orphanage newly opened at Fufeng. It was three days journey on a train but Gladys didn't care anymore. She was too ill to count the days.

Fufeng was a big, dirty city. At the orphanage the children ate bread and they hated it. Mountain people only ate millet and maize. Still, they were no longer going to be hungry, thirsty, tired or in danger.

Gladys stayed at the Christian Mission with her own adopted children. Everyone was eager to know her story and she was invited to visit a village some distance away to give a talk.

She went with two of the Mission women but as she walked, her feet refused to go where she wanted. At the village, when she was given food, she couldn't hold the chopsticks. yet she had used them for ten years. When she did control them she couldn't raise the food to her mouth. She complained of a headache and was taken to lie down.

She remembered nothing else. For weeks she raged in a fever. The missionaries sent her back to Sian to the hospital but Gladys didn't know where she was or even who she was. She had fever, pneumonia and typhus – the result of starvation, exhaustion, depression, too much walking, sleeping on damp ground and wearing damp, dirty clothes.

She didn't die and the doctor said, 'There can be only one reason for her getting better– God has more work for her to do.'

After her recovery, her health stayed very poor for the rest of her life.

10 Two Homelands

Gladys was thirty-eight when she arrived at Fufeng with the orphans. It was April 1940.

The Japanese were advancing and taking over all of China, pushing the Nationalists further and further south into a small corner of the country.

After she left Tsehchow, David Davies was captured as a spy. He was tortured and kept prisoner until the end of the war. Jean Davies and her children were sent to another prison.

In Europe there was war and Britain was being bombed. Gladys knew nothing of all this. During her illness her temperature was often 105 degrees for days. This had a terrible effect on her mind and in the following years the fever kept coming back.

Friends asked the British Consul to get her back to England but they had no power to do this. Gladys May Aylward from London, England was Ai weh-deh, Chinese citizen.

Her children were all at school and when she was better she needed to work to provide for them. She took a job in a leper colony. Until then the lepers, like the convicts in Yangcheng prison, had lived without hope. Ai weh-deh soon cheered their hearts with her love and kindness.

She continued her missionary work outside, too, but it wasn't as hard as when she first went to China. Other missionaries had already been to the outlying villages and many people had been converted to Christianity.

She knew the name of every orphan she'd brought safely across the Shansi mountains and as they grew up and moved away, they all wrote to Ai weh-deh. Some even called her Auntie Glad.

As the years went by, Ninepence married and the others became teachers, ministers or soldiers.

In 1942 Japan went to war with America and Europe. It ended in 1945 and the war between China and Japan ended at the same time, long before Sian could be captured.

Then the Communists began to take a strong hold on the country and they hated the Christians. They were as cruel to them as the Japanese had been. Gladys saw many of her friends and the grown-up orphans killed or taken off to concentration camps. Her son, Less, became a Nationalist soldier and was shot by the Communists.

Seven years after that long, distressing walk to safety, an American missionary was introduced to Gladys. He asked how long she had worked in China. She told him seventeen years. Where had she spent most of her time? She told him of the Inn of Eight Happinesses at Yangcheng, in the south of Shansi.

'Oh,' he said. 'Did you ever meet that little

English woman there known as Ai weh-deh?'

'That's me!' she replied.

He asked when she had last visited her family in England. She told him she had never been back to visit because there wasn't enough money for the fare. 'I'll never see them again,' she said sadly.

The missionary said nothing but he knew of an oganisation who helped in these cases. When he told them about Gladys, they gladly sent her the fare.

Mr and Mrs Aylward ran up and down the platform looking for 'Our Glad'. Had she missed the train to London? Had she fallen ill again on the journey?

Soon all the passengers left the station - all except one elderly little Chinese lady who stood gazing about her, looking lost. She wore a long Cheong Sam (Chinese dress). Her greying, black hair was pulled back from her face and tied into a severe bun at the back of her head. She peered through horn-rimmed glasses at Rosina and Thomas Aylward. Suddenly recognition dawned and they all fell into each other's arms.

She had always been thin but now she looked drawn, haggard and older than her own mother. It wasn't the same Gladys they'd waved off all those years before in her bright red coat and dress, with so much hope shining in her eyes.

When she spoke it was in Chinese and it took months for her to remember to speak English all the time.

Her family fussed over her, nursing her back to health. Gadys was surprised at the number of letters and callers she received. Then she learned that while she had been preaching Christianity in China, her mother had been giving talks at schools and churches about 'The Work Our Gladys Is Doing In China'.

She was quite famous and didn't know it. Reporters came to interview her. The BBC were doing a series about war heroes and Gladys had first hand experience of war in China. Then there was a radio play based on her life.

An author, Alan Burgess, wrote her life story and called it *The Small Woman*. Eventually a film was made about her called, *Inn Of The Sixth Happiness*. Maybe you have seen it on television.

Her next ten years were spent travelling round England and Europe, lecturing and preaching. She met the Queen and the Duke of Edinburgh and in Europe she met the head of every state she visited.

The girl who once came fifty-third in her school class, and was later rejected by China Inland Mission became one of the best known missionaries the world has ever known.

In England she founded the Gladys Aylward Charitable Trust for orphans.

She helped to establish a hostel in Liverpool, in the north of England, for the Chinese who lived there and for visiting Chinese seamen. Before World War II, 6,000 Chinese lived in an area of Liverpool called Chinatown. During the heavy bombing it was badly damaged and many lost their lives. When the Communists took over power in China, lots of Chinese left the country and many came to join relatives and friends in

Liverpool. They were in a strange land and Gladys remembered how she had felt when she first went to their country. The hostel would be a meeting place for them all and would help the newcomers to settle down and feel at home.

All this work took a lot of her energy and each talk she gave upset her as she recalled all the horrors and cruelty she'd seen.

From letters from her adopted children she learned of refugees in Hong Kong who needed clothing. She set up jumble sales for funds and got friends to collect clothes to send to them.

In the letters from China she heard of how the Communists were having mass executions and she worried for the race she'd come to love so much. She'd heard nothing of Ninepence for two years and didn't know if she were still alive. Ninepence was alive and had a little boy yet Gladys didn't know that she was a grandmother.

When she had come to England Gladys had been asked to report to her local police-station at regular intervals because, as a Chinese citizen, she was an alien.

Eventually, like Jeannie Lawson all those years earlier, Gladys felt she must return to China and she began to make arrangements.

A threatening letter arrived saying that death awaited her if she went back but she was determined.

On the 15th of April, 1957, Gladys May Aylward said farewell to her family again and sailed for the British island of Hong Kong, situated at the foot of China's mainland.

She had money now, from her lectures and the

film – enough to enable her to help the Chinese people – but in what way? She didn't know where to go. Communist China's mainland was closed to her, although Ninepence and many of the orphans lived there.

One of her orphans, Michael, was a minister living in Hong Kong. He wanted to be a missionary.

'Why don't we open a Mission and a school?' Gladys said. They did and it became the famous Hope Mission.

The Nationalist government had settled in Formosa (now called Taiwan), an island off the south-east mainland, and Gladys heard of more work for her there.

The Chinese have two languages – Mandarin and Cantonese, each with many dialects. The government wanted everyone to learn Mandarin as it would be more convenient if all the refugees could understand each other. In Shansi Gladys had learned Mandarin and she was delighted to take on the task of teaching it.

Off she went to Formosa, to travel all over the island to schools, colleges, churches and even prisons.

One day she arrived back at the house where she stayed. She was exhausted and longed for sleep. But there in her room she found a tiny, abandoned baby – left for her to take care of.

'Oh, I'm much too old to take babies again,' she said to Jesus, the friend she knew was beside her. 'Babies belong to young mothers. I'm fifty-five and I have my teaching to do.'

She had a neighbour she could trust and she

took the baby to her, offering to pay for its keep. As she left she said, 'If any more arrive, will you take them too?'

Dozens arrived, orphaned, lost or abandoned. Ai weh-deh took them all and gave up her teaching. But often she felt too old and tired to play with them. 'If only there was someone younger to help me,' she thought and remembered that Jeannie Lawson had said those very words.

At this time she was being asked to travel the world, giving talks in America – Canada – New Zealand – Australia – Korea – back to England and, of all places – Japan. The Japanese Emperor had declared that the Shinto religion was wrong to treat him like a god and to teach that doing wrong could be right. From then on many Japanese became Christians.

The Gladys Aylward Orphanage was opened in Formosa and within days it held a bei of children.

Gladys was sixty and felt too old for the work. She was the right age to be a grandmother but the wrong age for a mother and she asked Jesus for help.

First, Kathleen Langton arrived from Nottingham, England, and next a very wealthy man came saying he was opening a very big orphanage and was looking for children to fill it!

Gladys was so relieved. She sent all the older children there and kept only twenty tiny babies for herself and Kathleen to care for.

Her adopted family and the Shansi orphans were spread far and wide across the globe and at sixty Gladys was grandmother and Auntie Glad to hundreds of people.

On New Year's morning, 1970, just one month before her sixty-eighth birthday, she awoke with a streaming cold. Kathleen begged her to stay in bed but Gladys insisted on going to give a promised talk to some soldiers' wives at the American army base.

When she got home she was so tired that she went to bed without anything to eat. Kathleen sent for the doctor and he gave her an injection. He said she had flu and must stay in bed.

A little later, Kathleen took her a hot drink. She smiled at the way her patient had tossed and turned, throwing the bed clothes on to the floor. She picked them up and tucked them in round the sleeping Ai weh-deh. But when Kathleen touched her she knew that all Gladys' hard work for her dear Lord was finally over - Ai weh-deh was dead.

One of the babies asleep in another bed across the room stirred in his sleep. Kathleen picked him up and tip-toed from the room.

Unlike that of Jeannie Lawson, Ai weh-deh's body was placed in a glass topped coffin and given a 'lying in state'. More than 1,000 people went to her funeral service and other memorial services were held all over the world.

Her body now lies in a marble tomb on a hill in the garden of Christ's College at Taipei, the capital of Taiwan. The garden overlooks the estuary facing the mainland of China – in the direction of Yangcheng and the Inn of Eight Happinesses where once hung a card saying: